UNDERSTANDING
Our
CATHOLIC NEIGHBORS

UNDERSTANDING
Our
CATHOLIC NEIGHBORS

MATHEW SCHMALZ
& ALONZO L. GASKILL

CFI
An imprint of Cedar Fort, Inc.
Springville, Utah

© 2023 John A. & Leah D. Widtsoe Foundation
All rights reserved.

No part of this book may be reproduced in any form whatsoever, whether by graphic, visual, electronic, film, microfilm, tape recording, or any other means, without prior written permission of the publisher, except in the case of brief passages embodied in critical reviews and articles.

This is not an official publication of The Church of Jesus Christ of Latter-day Saints. The opinions and views expressed herein belong solely to the author and do not necessarily represent the opinions or views of Cedar Fort, Inc. Permission for the use of sources, graphics, and photos is also solely the responsibility of the author.

Paperback ISBN 13: 978-1-4621-4645-1
Ebook ISBN 13: 978-1-4621-4662-8

Published by CFI an imprint of Cedar Fort, Inc.
2373 W. 700 S., Suite 100, Springville, UT 84663
Distributed by Cedar Fort, Inc., www.cedarfort.com

LIBRARY OF CONGRESS REGISTRATION NUMBER: 2023942344

Cover design by Shawnda Craig
Cover design © 2023 Cedar Fort, Inc.

Printed in the United States of America
10 9 8 7 6 5 4 3 2 1
Printed on acid-free paper

Contents

Preface vii
Foreword ix

SECTION 1: ROMAN CATHOLIC BELIEFS AND DOCTRINES

1. Overview of Roman Catholic Beliefs and Doctrines 3
2. Beliefs Shared by Roman Catholics and Latter-day Saints ... 11
3. Differences between Latter-day Saint and Catholic Beliefs ... 17
4. Appreciation for Unique Roman Catholic Beliefs and Doctrines ... 25

SECTION 2: ROMAN CATHOLIC RELIGIOUS PRACTICES

5. Overview of Roman Catholic Religious Practices 31
6. Practices Shared by Roman Catholics and Latter-day Saints ... 41
7. Differences between Latter-day Saint and Roman Catholic Practices ... 47
8. Common Misperceptions of Catholicism 53
9. Appreciation for Roman Catholic Religious Practices 57

SECTION 3: INTERFAITH DIALOGUE

10. Latter-day Saint Engagement with Roman Catholicism 63
11. Best Practices for Interfaith Dialogue with Roman Catholics ... 67
12. Appreciation for Latter-day Saint Beliefs and Practices 75

APPENDICES

Glossary of Catholic Terms 81
Important Dates and Events in Catholicism 88
Important Catholic Figures 90
Significant Locations in Roman Catholicism 92
Catholic Prayers and Creedal Statements 93
Chart Comparing Catholic and Latter-day Saint Doctrine 95
Suggested Readings on Roman Catholicism 98

About the Authors 101

PREFACE

The *Understanding Our Neighbors* series is designed to help members of The Church of Jesus Christ of Latter-day Saints become better neighbors and friends with those of other faiths. As the title of this series suggests, our goal is to understand others better so we can stand together with them in matters of faith, support and defend them in times of need, and rejoice in the mutual discovery of deep friendship. Such genuine love, support, and commitment are at the heart of what is often called interfaith dialogue.

The purpose of the *Understanding Our Neighbors* series is to provide an example of meaningful interfaith dialogue so that Church[1] members can better appreciate the faith and traditions of our neighbors, their commitment to God, and how they seek to honor Him. Efforts to convert others, no matter how sincere or well-intentioned, are incompatible with this effort to create community understanding and appreciation. While Latter-day Saints often focus on our responsibility to preach the gospel, interfaith dialogue serves a different purpose—it is a meaningful, two-way conversation where both Latter-day Saints and our neighbors of other faiths learn from one another and leave more committed to and excited about their own religion. Having been strengthened spiritually, we can both find ways to work together in common causes of righteousness and go forth to bless the world in our own unique and inspired ways.

---

1. In this book, we use the capitalized term "Church" to refer to The Church of Jesus Christ of Latter-day Saints and the lowercase "church" to refer to other faith communities. This differentiation is meant as a sort of shorthand and does not imply that other religious groups are less valuable to God's work in the world.

We encourage all people of faith to make every effort to draw closer to God. We hope this series can help each of us to take our religious commitments more seriously, to live holier lives, and to be better religious neighbors.

The John A.& Leah D. Widtsoe Foundation

Foreword

This project grew out of a statement from Elder Dieter F. Uchtdorf about an article in a German newspaper telling its readers what Mormons believe. "They ought to ask us to tell their readers what we believe," he remarked. That got me thinking: Why not ask a scholar of another faith to write a short booklet about their religion, tailored for a Latter-day Saint audience? Then, why not ask a Latter-day Saint scholar to join in writing the booklet to show what this means to Latter-day Saints, what our commonalities are, and how and why we differ? This way, our work will be accurate from both traditions.

The outreach of The Church of Jesus Christ of Latter-day Saints over the past decade has been remarkable. As it continues to expand the world's understanding of its doctrine, mission, people, and culture, its membership is growing across the globe. This means that the Church's "neighbors" are becoming ever more diverse in their beliefs, lifestyles, and ways of worship.

Asking the world to understand the Church and its people must be accompanied by asking our members to also understand our neighbors, friends, associates, and communities so that we are better neighbors as well. This presents a great opportunity for the John A. & Leah D. Widtsoe Foundation to fulfill its mission to serve as the Center for Global Latter-day Saint Leadership and Life in a very real and meaningful way by presenting this *Understanding Our Neighbors* series.

It is one thing to learn to tolerate one another, but it is even more important to understand and ultimately to appreciate one another—our similarities as well as our differences. This initiative aims to help our Latter-day Saint community both understand and appreciate our neighbors of other faiths so that we can work together to accomplish God's purposes in the world. We hope this series will become standard reading in all of our communities throughout the world and will help us all to answer the lawyer's question: "And who is my neighbor?" (Luke 10:29).

Larry L. Eastland, PhD
Chair & President, John A. & Leah D. Widtsoe Foundation

SECTION 1
Roman Catholic Beliefs and Doctrines

This section focuses on Roman Catholic beliefs and doctrines, explaining how they are similar to and different from the beliefs and doctrines of The Church of Jesus Christ of Latter-day Saints (which, to avoid long repetition, will sometimes be referred to here as the Church of Jesus Christ). The section is structured as a meaningful interfaith dialogue: teaching basic concepts, finding common ground, discussing differences, and ending with words of appreciation for unique Roman Catholic beliefs and doctrines.

1

Overview of Roman Catholic Beliefs and Doctrines

By Dr. Mathew N. Schmalz

Beginnings of Roman Catholicism

Catholics trace their faith's origin to Jesus Christ identifying Simon Peter as the apostle who would lead His church. In Matthew 16:18, Jesus says, "And I say also unto thee, That thou art Peter, and upon this rock I will build my church; and the gates of hell shall not prevail against it."[1]

In addition to using the word "church" (*ecclesia*), the original Greek plays on the word *Petros*, the word translated as "Peter," which is related to the word *petra*, which means "rock." Thus, for Catholics, Peter is the "rock" on which the Church would be built.

---

1. The translation here is from the King James Bible, which is more familiar to Latter-day Saints. Catholics usually use the New American Bible. In the New American Bible the lines read, "And so I say to you, you are Peter, and upon this rock I will build my church, and the gates of the netherworld shall not prevail against it." See The New American Bible, http://www.vatican.va/archive/ENG0839/__PVP.HTM.

Catholics believe that Peter was the first pope,[2] the vicar or representative of Christ, and the other apostles were considered to be the first bishops.[3] After the death of the apostles, "bishop" was the title applied to leaders of geographical areas called dioceses. Dioceses were smaller communities at first, but over time they became large enough to have the same boundaries as local Roman municipalities or cities.

The historical record indicates that the bishop of Rome—understood as the successor to Peter—was speaking authoritatively as early as the reign of Clement (from about AD 91 onward). By this time, Christianity was recognized as a religion distinct from Judaism, and Christians were not allowed to attend synagogue services. In addition, a separate clergy,[4] as distinct from the laity,[5] was charged with performing rituals (called sacraments[6] in Catholicism) having a special spiritual power and impact.[7]

Catholic Beliefs and Doctrines

Overall, the Catholic system of belief is complex, and it is relatively rare to find members of Catholic laity who know and understand all the various subtleties associated with Church doctrine. Like many Christian denominations, the Catholic Church accepts basic creedal statements such as the Apostles' Creed[8] and the Nicene Creed.[9] For the Catholic Church, the two fundamental sources of God's revelation—and so Catholic doctrine—are scripture and tradition. "Scripture" is understood as the Old Testament

---

2. The spiritual and administrative head of the Catholic Church on earth. The pope is considered to be the successor of the apostle Peter and the representative of Christ.
3. The leader of an administrative district called a diocese. Bishops are chosen by the pope.
4. Ordained ministers such as bishops, priests, and deacons, who have authority to administer the sacraments.
5. Non-ordained or non-consecrated members of the Catholic Church; often called "the faithful" or "the people of God."
6. A ritual or sign instituted by Christ that provides grace.
7. For a brief overview of significant events in Catholic history, see "Important Dates and Events in Catholicism" in the appendices.
8. One of the earliest statements of Christian doctrine, traditionally believed to express the beliefs of the apostles. It affirms faith in God, the Father; Jesus, the Son; and the Holy Spirit.
9. The creed that summarizes the orthodox faith of Catholicism and is used in the liturgy of most Christian churches. It was adopted at the first Council of Nicaea in AD 325.

(including what are called deuterocanonical or Apocryphal books[10]) and the New Testament. "Tradition" is how the Church has interpreted scripture through its theologians and its authoritative interpreters, the bishops and the pope.

The Magisterium

In the Catholic Church, the authority to teach and define doctrine is called the magisterium. It is divided into two basic parts: extraordinary and ordinary. The extraordinary magisterium refers to special and specific pronouncements made by the pope or through a council convened and sanctioned by him. Teachings of the extraordinary magisterium are considered to be infallible and necessary for salvation.[11] The extraordinary magisterium builds on the ordinary magisterium. The ordinary magisterium is not necessarily infallible but can contain infallible truths of the Catholic faith if a particular doctrine is taught consistently over time by the bishops of the entire church in communion with the pope. In addition to indicating a lower level of clarity and authority, "ordinary" also refers to "ordinary" transmissions of teachings surrounding faith and morals such as papal letters, called encyclicals. The magisterium, both extraordinary and ordinary, also listens to, and evaluates, what is called the sensus fidelium or the sense of the faithful, which refers to the collective understanding of elements of the Catholic faith by members of the Church, from bishops to laity, over time.

In addition to beliefs contained in the extraordinary and/or ordinary magisterium, another category of beliefs is subject to prudential judgment, where individuals might in good faith and conscience weigh a particular issue differently and come to different conclusions. For example, questions concerning the appropriate level and means of supporting the poor would generally fall under the category of prudential judgment, even though

---

10. Literally "second canon," these are parts of the Old Testament accepted as authentic by the Catholic and Greek Orthodox Churches but not by many other Christian denominations. These books are also called the Apocrypha and include the books of Tobit, Judith, Baruch, Sirach, 1 Maccabees, 2 Maccabees, and Wisdom of Solomon, as well as additions to Esther and Daniel.
11. A pronouncement incapable of being erroneous, as when a pope speaks ex cathedra or "from the throne" regarding a question of faith or morals. Infallibility is also understood to apply to proclamations made by councils of the entire Church.

helping the poor is an essential and consistent part of the Catholic Church's magisterium.

The Trinity

The Catholic understanding of God is expressed in the doctrine of the Trinity, in which there is only one God but three Persons: the Father, the Son, and the Holy Spirit. Traditionally, the Son and the Holy Spirit are described as "one-in-being" with the Father, who is equally divine. The distinction between the three Persons lies in their eternal interrelationship. The Father begets the Son, and the Holy Spirit proceeds from both the Father and the Son. Neither the Son nor the Holy Spirit are created by the Father at a single point in time, but each shares in the fulness of the divinity that constitutes the one eternal God who acts in the world.

Jesus Christ is understood to be the incarnate Son of God, fully human and fully divine. Jesus was conceived by the power of the Holy Spirit and born of the Virgin Mary. He was crucified under the rule of the Roman governor Pontius Pilate, died, and rose again from the dead. Catholics believe that salvation comes through Jesus Christ and His loving self-sacrifice for the sins of human beings. The Holy Spirit, who proceeds from the Father and Son together, is usually associated with the ongoing sanctification of the Church in its liturgy,[12] preaching, and teaching.

Mary

Mary is called "the Mother of God" in the Catholic tradition. While Mary was fully human, she is understood to have been immaculately conceived, which means that she was born without the stain of original sin.[13] In Catholic doctrine, she conceived Jesus by the power of the Holy Spirit and remained a virgin throughout her life. As was proclaimed by Pope Pius XII in 1950, Mary was "assumed body and soul into heavenly glory" after her

---

12. The set of rituals including the celebration of Mass and the other sacraments; the formula for public worship of God and proclamation of the gospel.
13. The disposition to sin inherent in all human beings, inherited as a consequence of the disobedience of Adam and Eve in the Garden of Eden.

earthly life completed its course.[14] The twin dogmas[15] of the Immaculate Conception and the Assumption are thus special marks of Catholic understandings of Mary's significance in God's plan for human salvation.

The Church

In the Catholic tradition, the Church has been presented or conceptualized in a variety of ways: broadly, it denotes the unity of all Christians; it also means "the body of Christ" or the "people of God." Fundamentally, the Catholic Church is a living community and institution willed by God for proclaiming the gospel and enabling the salvation of human beings. As the body of Christ, the Church is, in a special way, the presence of Christ in the world today. The Church's earthly leader is the pope, who is understood to be the successor to the apostle Peter, who, in turn, was specifically identified by Jesus Christ to head the Church. The pope is understood to teach infallibly concerning faith and morals under the very specific condition of speaking *ex cathedra*. Literally "from the throne," this term refers to the pope consciously invoking his authority as vicar (or representative) of Christ. Under the pope are the bishops, who are understood to be successors of the apostles.

Priests and deacons are ordained by bishops. Some priests lead a parish, an established local community within a wider geographical jurisdiction called a diocese, which is headed by a bishop. Deacons can assist both priests and bishops in administrative and some liturgical responsibilities. Bishops may administer all of the seven sacraments (explained below); priests have the authority to administer most of them, depending on the circumstances.

The laity also have specific rights and responsibilities. Qualified laity may assist clergy in advisory roles in the parish, as lectors[16] during services, and in Church councils. As laypeople go about their lives in the world, they are required to conform their conduct—and their conscience—to the

---

14. Pope Pius XII, Munificentissimus Deus: Defining the Dogma of the Assumption, Nov. 1, 1950, http://www.vatican.va/content/pius-xii/en/apost_constitutions/documents/hf_p-xii_apc_19501101_munificentissimus-deus.html.
15. A binding, divinely revealed truth, associated with a decree made by a council of the whole Church or an ex cathedra statement of the pope in which infallibility is invoked.
16. A reader during worship, often a layperson.

teaching authority of the Church. As their means allow, members of the laity are also required to materially support the Church.

Sacraments

Catholics celebrate several kinds of rituals; as a group, these are called the liturgy of the Church. Over time, seven of these liturgical rites, called sacraments, have become the most significant. By the traditional definition, sacraments are outward signs, instituted by Christ, to give grace.[17]

While the specific sacraments are detailed in the section on Catholic religious practices, the sacraments themselves shed light on the structure of Catholicism. In the Church, belief is often expressed through, and confirmed by, ritual. The sacraments are not a ritualized way to automatically receive grace. Rather, their efficacy relies in part upon the faith and belief of the individual receiving them. In addition, the ritual structure of Catholicism depends on a particular class of people, priests, who are specially authorized to perform the sacraments. Sacraments thus reflect the Catholic belief in the Church as a divinely established institution that enables sanctification and salvation, in part, through liturgical rites as well as through private prayer and ethical action.

Saints

Contrary to a common misconception, Catholics do not worship saints or the Virgin Mary—they venerate them and may ask for their intercession. In Catholicism, the title "saint" is applied posthumously to certain people who have led a life of heroic virtue during their earthly lives. In this context, "heroic virtues" has the very specific meaning of exemplifying the four cardinal virtues of prudence, temperance, fortitude, and justice, as well as the theological virtues: faith, hope, and charity.

The process for being named a saint in the Catholic Church is called canonization, the word "canon" meaning an authoritative list. A diocese brings a cause, or case, before the Vatican office in charge of considering candidates for sainthood. After their extensive investigation, with briefs that detail the examination of the candidate's life and writings, the final decision

---

17. The unmerited help that God provides human beings to draw close to Him.

lies with the pope. If he signs a Decree of Heroic Virtue, the person becomes venerable. Then two stages remain: beatification and sainthood. If it can be confirmed that one miracle has been performed through the intercession of the venerable individual, they advance in rank to beatification, or "blessed."[18] If a second miracle is confirmed, the blessed becomes a saint. In such cases, intercession is understood to mean "the aid of" prayers given on our behalf by the venerable, blessed, or saint. However, a miracle is always understood to be fundamentally a gift of God, who alone is worshipped. Persons who are named saints are listed on the Catholic liturgical calendar and given a special day, called a feast.

Social Teaching

There is a long tradition of Catholic social teaching on the proper organization and orientation of society. This social teaching has two overarching themes: the dignity of human life and the common good. The Catholic Church understands life as a precious gift from God. This belief informs Catholic opposition to abortion, capital punishment, and euthanasia. Furthermore, artificial means of conception and contraception are prohibited under Catholic doctrine because they interrupt and even distort the natural—and divinely blessed—giving between husband and wife that brings forth new life.

The common good refers to ideals of general welfare that should determine the proper distribution of resources as well as human works and labor. In making such a determination, a primary obligation is reaching out in justice and charity to the poor and those who suffer. In specific regard to social organization, the Catholic Church affirms the importance of private property, but private property must be held to serve the greater good. The Catholic Church has supported taxation as a means to justly distribute wealth and the right of workers to organize.

In recent years, two aspects of serving the common good have assumed renewed significance in Catholicism: care for the environment and the

---

18. One level below sainthood. A blessed is someone who led a life of heroic virtue and by whose intercession one miracle has taken place. Martyrs and confessors (those who were put to death or tortured for their faith) do not need a miracle associated with them to become blessed. The process for being named "blessed" is called "beatification."

concept of subsidiarity. Fundamental to serving the common good is protecting the environment, since natural creation is considered to be good and essential to human flourishing. The principle of subsidiarity holds that nothing should be done by a complex organization or means that can be accomplished by a simpler organization or means. Debate over the proper scope of governmental involvement in society and human affairs has become a crucial feature of contemporary Catholicism.

Afterlife

The Catholic Church, along with many other Christian traditions, teaches that at the Second Coming of Christ, all will be raised from the dead for a final judgment. (By contrast, in Latter-day Saint theology the Second Coming is neither the time of a universal resurrection nor the day of final judgment.) Like many other Christian denominations, the Catholic Church affirms the reality of both heaven and hell. Within the Catholic tradition, hell has been conceptualized in many different ways. For example, it has often been seen as a place of eternal torment by fire, as depicted in scriptural imagery. The more contemporary understanding of hell is existence without God—an agonizing condition, to be sure, but one that lacks the specific punishments once associated with "hellfire."

Heaven too has been conceptualized in a number of ways. Relying again on images from the scriptures, it is seen as a place of light, refreshment, and peace. The most enduring image of heaven is one of eternal contemplation of God's love and beauty, which is called "the beatific vision."[19]

Catholic tradition has also developed a belief in the existence of an intermediate state of purification, called purgatory, before the last judgment. After death, each person's soul will be judged immediately in the particular judgment. Those who have died without making a final confession may first need to do penance for any residual offenses. Purgatory, then, is that state of purgation in which the last traces of sin are removed and the soul purified to enter heaven and the presence of God.

---

19. "Immediate knowledge" or vision of God experienced in heaven by those who are saved.

2

Beliefs Shared by Roman Catholics and Latter-day Saints

By Dr. Alonzo L. Gaskill

Perhaps because of antagonism between these two traditions in the past, members of The Church of Jesus Christ of Latter-day Saints often do not think of their religion as having much in common with Roman Catholicism. In fact, during the first half of the twentieth century, members often defined themselves by how they differed from Catholics. However, the two faith traditions share many similarities in doctrine and belief. What follows is a sampling of those parallels.

Salvation through Christ

Both the Catholic and Latter-day Saint traditions teach that salvation is to be found in and through Jesus Christ. Both denominations are clear that, without Jesus's grace and manifest mercy, all would be lost—as no human will ever be able to do sufficient good works to merit her or his own salvation. Thus, Catholics and Latter-day Saints have a very Christ-focused doctrine of salvation. Jesus—and Jesus alone—is the source of salvation in both traditions. Because both Roman Catholicism and the Church of Jesus Christ teach that their sacraments or ordinances are a means of receiving Christ's grace, Protestants have criticized both religions for believing in salvation by works instead of salvation by grace. This Protestant critique is incorrect, but it may be the result of members of both traditions who wrongly believe that they *are* saved by their own works. (Perhaps the mutual misunderstanding of our members on this vital point is one more parallel between the two traditions.)

In both Roman Catholic and Latter-day Saint doctrine, works—including sacraments or ordinances—are important because they prepare and enable us to access Christ's grace. However, in both traditions, the efficacy of any rite is found in Christ's grace and the participant's faith in that grace. Consequently, if one participates in a Catholic sacrament or Latter-day Saint ordinance but has no faith in Christ or His power to sanctify through that rite, it has no power. Jesus is the source of the power behind the covenants and commandments in both traditions. In this regard, Latter-day Saint Christians are closer to Roman Catholics than they are to the beliefs of most Protestant churches.

Revelation

Many Protestants hold to a position of *sola scriptura*—or scripture alone—as the source of divine revelation to the Church. In this view, one needs no revelation or divine guidance outside of what is found in the Bible. However, Roman Catholics and Latter-day Saints each see scripture and tradition as going hand in hand—both being a source of revelation *for* the Church and coming *to* the Church through its appointed leaders. Catholics interpret "tradition" to be the various councils of the Church and also the longstanding teachings of the faith. In the Church of Jesus Christ, tradition might be defined as longstanding teachings of modern-day prophets and apostles, along with various proclamations, official declarations, and occasional non-canonized discourses given by members of the First Presidency and Quorum of the Twelve Apostles. In both Catholic and Latter-day Saint belief, God does not limit Himself to speaking to the Church through ancient scripture alone. Rather, both faiths hold that God has continued to speak to and inspire members and leaders of the Church through various means, and these post-biblical revelations are as canonically authoritative as those found in the Bible—perhaps more so in their application to the times in which they are given.

Sacraments/Ordinances

While the Roman Catholic Church celebrates seven sacraments, in the Church of Jesus Christ only one ordinance or rite is officially called a sacrament—namely, the sacrament of the Lord's Supper (or Eucharist, as Catholics call it). That being said, since sacraments are by definition rites or ordinances that are symbols of a spiritual reality and that prepare the participant to access divine grace, the ordinances of The Church of Jesus Christ of Latter-day Saints considered salvific (or requisite for exaltation) qualify as sacramental. Baptism, confirmation, priesthood ordination, the endowment, and temple sealing all have a sacramental purpose and nature in the Church of Jesus Christ, as similar rites do in Roman Catholicism. In both traditions, these rites serve to connect the faithful with God in a covenant relationship, allow believers to access His mercy and grace, and help to develop the participant into a more holy being, manifesting more fully the image of God. Thus, sacramental ordinances serve similar purposes in the two traditions, and both faiths see engaging in such rites as having some influence on the salvation of the participant.

The Afterlife

While in times past, Catholics have perceived the ultimate destiny of the wicked as a place of "hellfire" and eternal torment, as has already been pointed out, most Catholics today would not think of it as such, and the Catholic Church's official position has shifted away from that view of the afterlife. The *Encyclopedia of Catholicism* states, "While the Church has canonized many saints, affirming that there are human beings in heaven, it has never affirmed that there is, in fact, a single human being in hell."[1] Thus, the common Christian mental image of the eternal abode of the unrighteous as being a place filled with the souls of the wicked being eternally tormented by hellfire simply does not fit in contemporary Roman Catholicism.

This accords with traditional Latter-day Saint beliefs about the afterlife and the eternal state of those who are not in the celestial kingdom. Latter-day Saint theology traditionally assumes that those who inherit the terrestrial or telestial kingdom, for example, are kept out of the presence of God

---

1. Richard P. McBrien, *The HarperCollins Encyclopedia of Catholicism* (San Francisco, CA: HarperSanFrancisco 1995), 608, S.v., "Hell," 608.

the Father for all eternity and do not enjoy the blessings of family kinship. To forever exist with the knowledge that one has forfeited the opportunity to be eternally with God and family would indeed be "hell." As Elder Jeffrey R. Holland of the Quorum of the Twelve Apostles stated, heaven "won't be heaven without my wife, and it will not be heaven without my children."[2]

That being said, even the lowest of the three degrees of glory is a place void of hellfire or eternal torment. The eighteenth-century Congregationalist Jonathan Edwards's concept of "sinners in the hands of an angry God" is foreign to contemporary Catholicism and to Latter-day Saints. In both traditions, God is a God of love—and even the worst reward in the hereafter will have no hint of a hell filled with fire.

Apostolic Succession and Priesthood Authority

In Roman Catholic and Latter-day Saint traditions, the doctrine of apostolic succession is foundational to each church's claim of priesthood authority. Contemporary Catholics see early Christian bishops as the successors to the apostles. Peter, the chief of the New Testament apostles, is believed by Catholics to have been the bishop of Rome. Thus, for Catholics, the New Testament office of apostle still exists today in Catholicism, but it does so in the form of the priesthood office of bishop. Consequently, Catholics describe the doctrine of apostolic succession as an unbroken line of bishops from the first century down to the twenty-first century Church. In this understanding, bishops have been on the earth since the foundation of Christianity, and there have always been apostolic keys and the apostolic office.

In Latter-day Saint belief, apostolic succession is seen as flowing into the Church of Jesus Christ in a different way, but with the same effect. Like Roman Catholics, Latter-day Saints believe that Jesus conferred on Peter— the chief or head apostle in the early New Testament church—all necessary priesthood keys. Upon Christ's passing, Peter led the Church through those keys as the earthly representative of, or "in the person of," Christ. As part of the "restitution of all things" (Acts 3:21) in "the dispensation of the fulness of times" (Doctrine and Covenants 27:13), the prophet Joseph Smith was directly ordained an apostle by Peter, James, and John, who themselves were ordained to that office by Jesus. Along with other angelic messengers,

---

2. Jeffrey R. Holland, interview, *The Mormons,* directed by Helen Whitney, PBS, 2007.

they conveyed to Joseph Smith all priesthood keys pertaining to this dispensation. Hence, even though there are nearly 1,800 years between the last New Testament apostle and Joseph Smith, apostolic succession is claimed by the Church of Jesus Christ through the immediate conveyance of the apostolic keys from Peter and others to Joseph Smith (similar to when Jesus received those keys in the New Testament—via their conveyance through deceased prophets). While Latter-day Saints do not see bishops as equivalent to apostles, they do see an unbroken line of apostles from Jesus to Peter to Joseph Smith, and down to the current president of the Church of Jesus Christ. With this shared view of the necessity of apostolic succession, Roman Catholics and Latter-day Saints stand out as unique, professing a position on divine priesthood that is not claimed by any Protestant denomination.

Related to the necessity of apostolic succession is the shared Catholic and Latter-day Saint belief in ecclesiastical (or church) hierarchy and ordained priesthood. In both faith traditions, Christ is seen as the head of the Church—but He has an earthly head whom He inspires and through whom He leads the Church. For Roman Catholics, this is the pope; for Latter-day Saints, it is the living prophet. As a result, both churches perceive God as continuing to lead and inspire the direction of the Church more than two thousand years after Jesus died. Both see God's hand manifest in the history of their respective movements. Both generally believe that God will not allow the mortal head of their church to lead the faithful astray on any issue necessary for their salvation. In both traditions, that singular earthly head, through his keys, grants some authority to local leaders of the Church, who are to act in their specific assignment with inspired leadership and ordained authority. Consequently, there is a "hierarchical leadership structure" in both traditions. The highest ecclesiastical leader is perceived by the faithful as speaking to and for God, but the local leader is also understood to have some measure of delegated stewardship, authority, and related inspiration—and Church members from the two traditions place their trust in both levels of authority.

3

Differences between Latter-day Saint and Catholic Beliefs

By Dr. Alonzo L. Gaskill

Although Catholicism and Latter-day Saint doctrines share a number of similarities, they also have differences. Some of these differences are significant, and others minor. What follows is a sampling of some of the more significant theological or doctrinal differences between the two faiths.

The Trinity/Godhead

When compared to most of the world's great religions, Christianity is distinctive in how it perceives Deity. Many non-Christians struggle to grasp the Christian perception of a Triune or Trinitarian God—but then, so do many Christians! Most Christian churches teach the doctrine of the Trinity, although their teachings vary. Indeed, what Protestants believe about the Trinity is not the same as what Eastern Orthodox Christians believe, and what the Orthodox teach about the nature of the Triune God is not the same as what Catholics teach. Additionally, some of the major denominations of Christianity, including Roman Catholicism, have members who understand this foundational doctrine differently than do their respective faith's theologians or leaders.

Despite the thousands of pages that have been published on the doctrine of the Trinity, most Christians would agree that, ultimately, God's nature is a mystery to the limited human mind. Even in the Church of Jesus Christ, it is understood that God is beyond full human comprehension. While Latter-day Saints acknowledge that their church has certain beliefs about God that other Christians do not know or believe, members of the Church of Jesus Christ also realize that the details of God's full nature are beyond any mortal comprehension.

Official Catholic doctrine teaches that the Father, Son, and Holy Spirit are one God existing in three Persons—simultaneously united in substance but utterly distinct in personhood.[1] Three separate Beings with a shared "essence" (sometimes rendered "nature") constitutes "God." In other words, the Father, Son, and Holy Spirit are perfectly united in all things, even though they are distinct Beings. Consequently, the three are called "one God." The "oneness" of the three Persons is emphasized to the degree that some Catholics erroneously view the three divine "Persons" as a singular "Being." This view is typically referred to as modalism, the belief that a single divine Being or Person appears in different modes or forms at different times—sometimes appearing as the Father, at other times as the Son, and at other times as the Holy Spirit. Catholicism officially rejects this view of the Trinity.

In the Church of Jesus Christ, the distinction between the Father, Son, and Holy Spirit is unmistakable, causing some outside of the faith to assume that Latter-day Saints are tritheists (worshippers of three gods) or polytheists (worshippers of many gods). In reality, Latter-day Saints worship the Father, in the name of the Son, through the Holy Spirit. This is more monotheistic or monolatrist than tritheistic. (The term "monolatrist" means one acknowledges the existence of other Deities but worships a singular God, specifically the Father in Latter-day Saint theology.[2]) Catholicism holds that the "shared essence" of the three distinct Persons of the Trinity constitute a singular God. In this relational conception of Deity, all three Persons of the Trinity are necessary in order for God to be God—not three Gods, but one God,

---

1. See Catherine Mowry Lacugna, "Trinity, Doctrine Of," in *The HarperCollins Encyclopedia of Catholicism*, Richard P. McBrien, editor (San Francisco, CA: HarperSanFrancisco 1995), 1271.
2. While some will say that the Saints worship *both* the Father and the Son, in scripture, Jesus clearly deflects worship of Himself onto His Father.

in three Persons, united in "essence" or nature. The *United States Catholic Catechism for Adults* explains:

> The mystery of the Holy Trinity is the central mystery of the Christian faith and life. God reveals himself as Father, Son, and Holy Spirit. The doctrine of the Trinity includes three truths of faith.
>
> First, the Trinity is One. We do not speak of three gods but of one God. Each of the Persons is fully God. They are a unity of Persons in one divine nature.
>
> Second, the Divine Persons are distinct from each other. Father, Son, and Spirit are not three appearances or modes of God, but three identifiable persons, each fully God in a way distinct from the others.
>
> Third, the Divine Persons are in relation to each other. The distinction of each is understood only in reference to the others. The Father cannot be the Father without the Son, nor can the Son be the Son without the Father. The Holy Spirit is related to the Father and the Son who both send him forth.[3]

In Latter-day Saint understanding, God includes both Father and Mother. There is no God the Father minus God the Mother, or vice versa. They are both fully divine in nature and utterly distinct Beings, and yet the sociality or relationship between the two allows for the functioning of their divine power. This is somewhat like the Catholic view of the Trinity—where God the Father, God the Son, and God the Holy Spirit constitute one God through their shared essence or nature and their relatedness, even though they are distinct Beings or Persons.

Regarding the third member of the Godhead, Roman Catholicism teaches what is traditionally referred to as the double procession of the Holy Spirit. In other words, most Catholics today believe that the Holy Spirit proceeds or issues forth from both the Father and the Son. For Catholics, if the Holy Spirit proceeds from the Father only, then the Son must be subordinate to the Father, a view contemporary Roman Catholics would see as heretical. The three members of the Trinity are understood to be coequal

---

3. *United States Catholic Catechism for Adults* (Washington, DC: U.S. Conference of Catholic Bishops, 2006), 52–53; available at https://www.usccb.org/sites/default/files/flipbooks/uscca/files/assets/basic-html.

and coeternal. The latter of these two terms means that the Father never existed at a time when the Son did not also exist. They have both been God throughout eternity—not two Gods but one God present in the three Persons or members of that Trinitarian Godhead.

In Latter-day Saint theology, by contrast, the Son is understood as having been spiritually "born" of the Father, doing nothing but what the Father gives Him to do (see John 5:19) and thus subordinating Himself to the Father. In this sense, the Father is the "senior" member of the Godhead who directs the work of the Son and the Holy Spirit. The *Encyclopedia of Mormonism* indicates that the Holy Ghost is a "spirit son of God the Father"—one of God's spirit "offspring."[4] Consequently, the Church of Jesus Christ does not see the three members of the Godhead as coequal or coeternal. The Son and the Holy Spirit owe their spiritual existence to God the Father and God the Mother, who brought them forth and gave them the ability to grow and progress (see Doctrine and Covenants 93:11–14). Thus, the Latter-day Saint theology of the Godhead would be seen as subordinationist in the eyes of Roman Catholic theologians. In the end, while there are similarities between the two traditions, the view of the Church of Jesus Christ with respect to the Godhead certainly differs in some fundamental ways from Roman Catholic understandings of the Triune God.

Original Sin

The Catholic Church has long had a doctrine of original sin. The essence of the doctrine is that because of what happened in Eden—as a consequence of Adam and Eve's disobediently partaking of the fruit, constituting humankind's first sin—all humans since that time have suffered significant and terrible consequences. This doctrine has been encapsulated in many ways by many scholars and authorities of the Catholic Church. Early in Catholic history, the emphasis was placed on our inheritance of Adam's guilt. Today, however, Roman Catholicism focuses more on the universal or collective "fallenness" of humans, and on the resulting terrible human condition that is traceable to Adam's choice in Eden. According to contemporary Catholic

---

4. See Stephen E. Robinson, "God the Father," in Daniel H. Ludlow, editor, *The Encyclopedia of Mormonism*, four volumes (New York: Macmillan, 1992), 2:548. See also Heber C. Kimball, "Faith in the Priesthood," in *Journal of Discourses*, 5:179; Joseph Fielding McConkie, "Holy Ghost," in Ludlow (1992), 2:649.

theologians, original sin has caused humans to lose the sanctifying grace God had intended for His creations. Adam and Eve's choice in the garden created a less than ideal human situation and was not what God hoped for His creations had they remained faithful.

In the Church of Jesus Christ, however, there is no doctrine of original sin. As the second article of faith indicates, Latter-day Saints do not believe that any person will be punished "for Adam's transgression." While the restored gospel acknowledges, with Catholicism, the "fallenness" of humans and the reality that "the natural man is an enemy to God" (Mosiah 3:19), the Church of Jesus Christ sees humankind's fallen condition as an intended part of the plan and necessary for their growth and eventual exaltation—not as an act that overturned God's ideal for His creations. Thus, the disagreement between Latter-day Saints and Roman Catholics on this subject is less about how the two interpret the influence of Adam and Eve's choice on the mortal experience and more about whether God intended for Adam and Eve to fall. Today, both faiths tend to see Adam and Eve's choice as causing a fallen earth and a difficult and tempting mortal experience. In contrast to Catholicism, however, Latter-day Saint theology holds that the Fall was part of the plan from the beginning—and the only way whereby God's children could become like Him (see Moses 5:11).

This understanding is the basis for the Latter-day Saint doctrine of free or moral agency. That agency was manifest in Adam and Eve choosing to enter this world from the garden, which resulted in each human having the opportunity to choose how we will live. The responsibility for our personal choices is placed on us rather than on Adam, whose transgression is more fully emphasized in Catholic theology.

Infallibility of Leaders

Another point of difference between the formal beliefs of Catholics and Latter-day Saints is the question of the infallibility of Church leaders. Although the subject of the pope's infallibility did not arise until the fourteenth century, Catholicism gradually became explicit in holding to the idea that Peter's successors, the popes, had the ability to teach doctrines and morals in an infallible way. At the First Vatican Council (1869–1870),[5] the

---

5. A council held in Rome, convened by Pope Pius IX and including bishops from the entire Church. The First Vatican Council proclaimed the dogma of papal infallibility.

Catholic Church declared the pope's "immunity from error." This immunity was understood to be a gift of the Holy Spirit by which the Church would always be protected from any fundamental or salvation-influencing errors on matters of faith or morality. Consequently, some Catholics today see the pope as infallible on *any* matter and at *all* times.

However, many Catholics hold that there are conditions to this immunity from error. In the view of some contemporary Catholic theologians, the pope has the ability to speak infallibly but, in order to do so, he needs to speak (1) *ex cathedra*, or authoritatively and officially as the head of the Church, (2) specifically on the subjects of faith or morality, and (3) with the intent of binding the whole Church by his decree. Thus, according to many Catholics, the pope is considered infallible only within parameters and context. The Second Vatican Council (1962–1965)[6] suggested that the pope could speak infallibly when within the parameters outlined above, and so too could the entire college of bishops when united on a given matter. Thus, infallibility in contemporary Catholicism is expressed in two ways: "extraordinary magisterium" (Latin *Deninire*), which is the infallibility of the pope and councils when exercising an official *judicium* or judgment (as Peter's rightful successor); or "ordinary magisterium" (Latin *Tradere*), which is the bishops speaking and teaching in unity throughout the world. Consequently, many Catholics today see infallibility as not as the sole purview of the pope but as a function and right of the Church as a collective body.

The question of the infallibility of the leadership of the Church of Jesus Christ is, in some ways, even more complex—in part because doctrine and culture sometimes merge. While, officially speaking, the Church of Jesus Christ does not teach that the prophets and apostles—including Peter, his successors, or those of any dispensation—are infallible, many members of the Church are prone to treat their words as such and may even expect perfection of the General Authorities (particularly the fifteen men who hold the apostolic office). That being said, Joseph Smith seemed uncomfortable with any attribution of infallibility toward him. He stated: "I told them I was but a man, and they must not expect me to be perfect; if they expected perfection from me, I should expect it from them, but if they would bear with my

---

6. A council of the entire Church convened by Pope John XXIII; also known as Vatican II. The Second Vatican Council established a more conciliatory posture to contemporary culture and allowed the Mass to be celebrated in local languages instead of Latin.

infirmities, and the infirmities of the brethren, I would likewise bear with their infirmities."[7] Joseph also said, "I never told you I was perfect,"[8] and "'A Prophet is not always a Prophet' only when he is acting as such."[9]

By contrast, Joseph's successors were sometimes more dogmatic in their teaching and leadership styles, Brigham Young being a prime example. The nuances of individual personalities and leadership styles led some Latter-day Saint prophets and apostles to speak in authoritative ways that could lead their followers to assume infallibility. Brigham Young, Joseph F. Smith, and Bruce R. McConkie, for example, each had a style of speech and an approach to doctrine that gave an air of infallibility to their words. That is not to imply that those men were speaking with the intent of being perceived as infallible. Nonetheless, their teachings (along with those of some other General Authorities with a similar teaching style) tended to be perceived more dogmatically than the teachings of men like John Taylor, George Albert Smith, David O. McKay, Howard W. Hunter, Gordon B. Hinckley, or Thomas S. Monson.

To summarize, both Roman Catholicism and the Church of Jesus Christ hold that God will not allow their respective church to get "off track" on any issue important for the salvation of their people. Nevertheless, whereas Roman Catholicism has an established means of enabling the pope or the Church to speak "infallibly," the Church of Jesus Christ claims no such formal procedure. The united voice of the First Presidency and the Quorum of the Twelve Apostles is seen as safe and reliable, but even in that context, they do not declare their collective or united pronouncements "infallible" or, in other words, that God cannot provide for differences in teachings or practices based on time and context, by giving ongoing revelation.

---

7. *Joseph Smith History*, 1838–1856, vol. D-1, 1414, https://www.josephsmithpapers.org/paper-summary/history-1838-1856-volume-d-1-1-august-1842-1-july-1843/57.
8. 12 May 1844, Joseph Smith, Sermon, Thomas Bullock Report, in *Words of Joseph Smith*, Andrew F. Ehat and Lyndon W. Cook, compliers (Provo, UT: Religious Studies Center, BYU, 1980), 369. See also https://www.josephsmithpapers.org/paper-summary/discourse-12-may-1844-as-reported-by-thomas-bullock/2
9. Joseph Smith, Journal, 8 Feb. 1843, https://www.josephsmithpapers.org/paper-summary/journal-december-1842-june-1844-book-1-21-december-1842-10-march-1843/178.

4

Appreciation for Unique Roman Catholic Beliefs and Doctrines

By Dr. Alonzo L. Gaskill

As someone comes to better understand another religious tradition, it is natural to develop an appreciation for the unique beliefs, ceremonies, or practices found in that tradition and to feel inspired or moved by them. This idea is sometimes referred to in interfaith dialogue as having holy envy. One might feel this sort of deep appreciation for a ritual or ordinance, a certain teaching, the musical tradition, the architecture of their houses of worship, or another aspect of a religion that is not part of the observer's own faith but which causes him or her to feel closer to God—and to wish his or her tradition had that element because of its inspiring nature. There are several things in Roman Catholicism for which a practicing Latter-day Saint Christian might have a holy envy; what follows is a discussion of just two examples.

Transubstantiation

Roman Catholicism has an important doctrine associated with the sacrament of the Lord's Supper known as transubstantiation. The word "transubstantiation" means literally "beyond the substance." In this Catholic doctrine, when the bread and wine of the sacrament are consecrated or blessed, they literally become the body and blood of Christ. Though they continue to look like bread and wine, in their substance or essence they are changed—and Jesus is literally present in the consecrated or blessed elements of bread and wine. For this reason, many Roman Catholics feel great awe or reverence when partaking of the sacrament of the Lord's Supper. If a member earnestly perceives the blessed bread and wine as literally Jesus's broken body and spilt blood, one can imagine the sense of reverence that would well up in the heart and mind of that member as she or he approaches the altar to receive these sacred and blessed elements.

While the restored gospel does not embrace the doctrine of transubstantiation, its contemplation can add meaning to Latter-day Saints' own sacrament of the Lord's Supper. If a Church member believed that the blessed bread and water in sacrament meeting had actually become Christ, it could profoundly affect how he or she prepares for the weekly ordinance. This preparation took on added importance in 2019 when the questions Church of Jesus Christ leaders ask to determine temple worthiness were updated to include, "Do you . . . prepare for and worthily partake of the sacrament?"[1] Often, it seems Latter-day Saints go to sacrament meeting without any element of preparation, having no specific sin they intend to repent of or no new commitment they intend to take up when they receive the symbols of Christ's broken body and shed blood. Latter-day Saints can make the sacred ordinance of the sacrament more meaningful in their lives by engaging in spiritual preparation, contemplation, and commitment as they partake. The act of eating the bread and drinking the water does not renew covenants in and of itself. Eating and drinking with *intent* renews covenants.

Prior to my conversion to The Church of Jesus Christ of Latter-day Saints, being then a believer in transubstantiation (or metousiosis), partaking of the sacrament of the Lord's Supper was an act of great awe for me. Members of The Church of Jesus Christ of latter-day Saints could do better at thinking about the remarkable reality that, when we partake with intent and focus, we quite literally reach back some two thousand years to Gethsemane and Golgotha and access Christ's atoning sacrifice; we access His remarkable gift of atonement. How can we take that lightly? The awe of transubstantiation is a reminder that you and I need to be more present and intentional when we partake of the Lord's Supper each week—because the most remarkable and sacred thing is happening as we place the bread in our mouths and press the cup to our lips. In this regard, there

---

1. "Church Updates Temple Recommend Interview Questions," 6 Oct. 2019, https://newsroom.churchofjesuschrist.org/article/october-2019-general-conference-temple-recommend.

is something powerful Latter-day Saints can learn from the Catholic understanding of the sacrament of the Lord's Supper.

Mediation and Intercession of Saints

Another doctrine of Catholicism that might be instructive for members of the Church of Jesus Christ has to do with the mediation or intercession of saints. Roman Catholics generally believe that the saints—those holy individuals who lived so faithfully that they now dwell in God's presence—have some power to intercede on behalf of mortals yet dwelling here on earth. While Catholics may have a variety of views on the matter, Catholicism officially teaches that prayers are answered only by God—and it is to God that appeals should be directed. However, saints may intercede with God as a means of gaining His favor on behalf of a mortal in need. Thus Catholics pray, "Holy Mary, Mother of God, *pray for us sinners*, now and at the hour of our death. Amen." Note that Mary is being asked to "pray for us," not to directly answer prayers herself—as that responsibility is God's and God's alone. In the general Catholic understanding, then, our righteous dead are aware of us and very concerned for us. Catholics generally feel a strong sense that the dead are active on their behalf—worried about their salvation and interacting with God for their benefit.

While Latter-day Saint Christians also have a connectedness with their dead, the emphasis is on how the living provide intercession for the dead by performing vicarious ordinances for them in temples. Latter-day Saints do not focus much on what the dead can do for the living. Yet, as President Joseph F. Smith taught, our family members who have died and gone to the spirit world "see us, they are solicitous for our welfare, they love us now more than ever."[2] Similarly, President George Albert Smith stated: "Those who are on the other side are . . . anxious about us. They are praying for us and for our success. They are pleading, in their own way, for their descendants, for their posterity who live upon the earth."[3] Along with focusing on redemption of their kindred dead, Latter-day Saints may find value in considering what the dead might be able to do for us from the other side of the veil (see Doctrine and Covenants 128:18).

---

2. Joseph F. Smith, in *Eighty-Sixth Annual Conference of the Church of Jesus Christ of Latter-day Saints* (Salt Lake City, Deseret News, 1906), 3.
3. *Teachings of the Presidents of the Church: George Albert Smith* (Salt Lake City: The Church of Jesus Christ of Latter-day Saints, 2011), 88.

SECTION 2
Roman Catholic Religious Practices

This section focuses on Roman Catholic religious practices and how they are similar to and different from those of The Church of Jesus Christ of Latter-day Saints. Like the last section, this section is structured as a meaningful interfaith dialogue: teaching basic concepts, finding common ground, discussing differences, explaining common misperceptions, and ending with words of appreciation for unique Roman Catholic religious practices. Important Catholic terms are defined in the text and collected in the glossary at the end of the book.

5

Overview of Roman Catholic Religious Practices

By Dr. Mathew N. Schmalz

The Seven Sacraments

In Catholicism, there are seven central rites, all instituted by Jesus while He was on earth: baptism, confirmation, holy orders, the Eucharist, matrimony, penance and reconciliation, and extreme unction. Through these sacraments Church members access the grace of God.

1. Baptism

The first and most important rite of initiation in Catholicism is baptism. The word "baptism" comes from the Greek word *bapto*, which means "to dip" or "to immerse." Baptism is most fundamentally an immersion in water, and in Judaism, baptism was the means by which adult converts were initiated into the faith. According to the Gospels, Jesus Himself was baptized by John the Baptist (see Mark 1:2–12; Matthew 3:1–17).

The early Catholic Church continued this tradition by baptizing initiates in "living water," such as rivers, and later in tubs or pools of water. These tubs or pools were eventually housed in a special eight-sided building called a baptistery, separate from the main church. Gradually, the Church practice shifted from adult to infant baptism. The reason for this was twofold: first, with the legalization of Christianity, most adults had already been baptized; second, infant mortality was high. Along with the change to infant baptism came the custom of pouring or sprinkling water over the infant instead of full immersion. Baptism was understood to be a crucial ritual because it was believed to be necessary for salvation, wiping clean the stain of the original sin of Adam and Eve's disobedience.

The contemporary Catholic rite of baptism takes place over a raised basin called a baptismal font, which is much smaller than ancient baptismal pools. Extended families and loved ones gather together, and often a godparent is chosen to sponsor and mentor the child in the faith throughout his or her life. The infant is presented over the font, and the priest makes the sign of the cross[1] (representing the Trinity) on the child's forehead. The parents and selected godparents are then asked to make a series of promises on the infant's behalf, rejecting Satan and professing belief in the Trinity. After promises are made, the priest anoints the child's forehead with oil and pours water over his or her head while repeating the formula, "I baptize you in the name of the Father, and of the Son, and of the Holy Spirit." After the baptism, white candles are lit, and the child is given a white garment to symbolize a new life in Christ.

2. Confirmation

While baptism is the preeminent rite of initiation in Catholicism, there is also confirmation, which strengthens or confirms a Catholic's faith. Confirmation was originally part of the baptismal rite when primarily adults were being baptized. However, with the shift to infant baptism, confirmation gradually became what it is today: a ceremony usually for those in their teen years, wherein the person participating in the confirmation rite is anointed with oil by a bishop after a period of preparation and study.

---

1. A gesture that symbolizes both the cross and the Trinity, made by outlining a cross from the forehead to the chest and to each shoulder while repeating, aloud or silently, "In the name of the Father, Son, and Holy Spirit."

3. Holy Orders

Priests who administer the sacraments must themselves pass through a ritual to move from the laity to their vocation as clergy. This sacrament is called "holy orders" or "ordination." After a period of seminary study, candidates for the priesthood are ordained into the diaconate, in which they serve as deacons. After a period in the diaconate, candidates are ordained into the priesthood through a rite that culminates in a bishop laying his hands upon them. This laying on of hands indicates that the candidates are now part of the apostolic succession, which can be traced back to Jesus Christ. Once ordained, a priest wears a stole for sacramental functions. A priestly stole is a piece of scarf-like cloth draped around the back of the neck of the officiating priest so that its two ends hang down in front. In the Roman Catholic Church, the priesthood is reserved for men because they are understood to symbolically represent Christ. Priests cannot be married, but widowers can become priests if they pledge not to remarry.

Bishops are priests who are selected to lead a diocese. Originally, bishops were chosen by the laity and clergy in their local municipality. Now bishops are selected by the Vatican in Rome, with the pope having final approval. Since bishops are already ordained priests, they go through another ceremony in which they are consecrated[2] or dedicated to their special leadership position. After consecration, bishops receive several important signs of their office for official functions: the crozier, a staff that brings to mind a shepherd's crook; and the miter, a pointed headdress with the two sides representing the Old and New Testaments. As part of their daily attire, bishops wear a cross on their chest—formally called a pectoral cross—as well as an episcopal ring and, often, a rose-colored skull cap called a zucchetto. Cardinals are bishops selected to be the Catholic Church's most senior officials. They are appointed by the pope and consecrated in a special ceremony at the Vatican. They are also involved in the choosing of a new pope. Cardinals, as their name suggests, wear scarlet for official functions.

Others in Catholicism, including nuns and some laypeople, live a consecrated life by making public vows of poverty, chastity, and obedience. While this does not represent holy orders as such, it does emphasize the roles of vows and renunciation within Catholic practice and spirituality.

---

2. Nuns, clergy, and laypersons who have taken a public vow of poverty, chastity, and obedience.

4. Eucharist

The central ritual of Catholicism is the Eucharist, or celebration of the Lord's Supper. This sacrament is officiated by a priest during the Mass. The word *eucharist* is of Greek origin and means "thanksgiving." The word "mass" comes from the Latin word *missa,* meaning "dismissal." It comes from what used to be the last words of the Mass celebrated in Latin: *Ite, missa est* or "Go, this is the dismissal." While the Mass is now performed in the common language of those who attend, the impact of the Latin remains in the terminology used for Catholic worship.

When a parishioner goes to Mass, they may first make the sign of the cross on their forehead with holy water, which has been specially blessed by a priest and is kept in a small basin at the entrance to the church. Parishioners then briefly kneel or genuflect[3] toward the tabernacle, a special container or dwelling place near the altar, in which the consecrated Eucharistic host[4] is kept. After taking her or his seat, the worshipper will find in the pew a booklet, called a missalette, which gives the words of the Mass. Most Catholics have the Mass memorized, but the missalette is still helpful, especially for visitors. When the priest enters, the congregation stands, and the priest makes the sign of the cross and begins the service.

The Mass has two parts. The first part is the liturgy of the Word, when the priest or a lector reads passages from the Old and New Testaments, which vary from week to week. The congregation stands for the reading from the Gospels but otherwise remains seated. Then comes a sermon called the homily, and the congregation stands for the recitation of the Nicene Creed. After the recitation is the prayer of the faithful, during which the congregation raises its prayers to God for the world, the Church, and the specific needs of members of the congregation.

The second part of the Mass is the liturgy of the Eucharist itself, commemorating the Last Supper that Jesus had with His disciples. During the liturgy of the Eucharist, the priest, who is understood to be acting in the person of Christ, repeats the Eucharistic prayer, drawn from Jesus's words in the New Testament. As the priest reads the words "Take this, all of you, and eat it: this is my body which will be given up for you," he elevates a Eucharistic host, a circular piece of unleavened bread. Then he elevates a

---

3. The act of lowering one's body by bending on one knee during worship.
4. A consecrated or blessed Eucharistic wafer, which is always made of unleavened bread.

wine chalice, which is made of precious metal, and says, "Take this all of you, and drink from it: this is the cup of my blood, the blood of the new and everlasting covenant." This prayer, and the rite associated with it, is called the consecration. During this phase of the Mass, members of the congregation kneel.

Catholics believe that when the elements of the Eucharist are consecrated, only the appearance of simple bread and wine remain because their inner essence has become the real body and blood of Jesus Christ. As previously explained, this change is known as transubstantiation. Thus, when Catholics celebrate the Eucharist, they do not experience it simply as a memorial of Jesus's life but as the real presence of His body and blood, soul and divinity.

The partaking of the bread and wine during the Mass is called Communion. After the consecration, congregants recite the Lord's Prayer ("Our Father") and then usually greet each other in the sign of peace, during which they shake each other's hand and say, "Peace be with you." At the conclusion of the Mass, congregants proceed to the altar for Communion. Only Catholics and members of Eastern Orthodox Churches are eligible to receive Communion. Today, the process for receiving Communion is to make a slight bow before accepting the Eucharistic host in the palm of the hand. Still, some people will receive Communion in the more traditional form, in which the priest places the Eucharistic host on the tongue. Often, congregants will also drink the consecrated wine from a common cup. Receiving the consecrated elements of the Eucharist represents a special way to commune with God. Individuals also commune with each other and express their union as members of the Church, which is also understood to be the body of Christ.

Catholics are expected to attend Mass every Sunday, although they are only required to receive the Eucharist during the Easter season. There are also daily masses throughout the year. Of all of the seven sacraments of the Church, the Eucharist is what draws Catholics together most consistently. There are also various ways of celebrating the Eucharist—called "rites"—which are equally Catholic but have diverse forms, structures, and traditions. For example, in India the Syro-Malabar Church celebrates the liturgy according to its own specific traditions while still being in full communion with (or fully accepted by) Church leadership in Rome.

5. Matrimony

Marriage—which, according to Catholic tradition, is only possible between one man and one woman—is another of the seven sacraments. Marriage is understood to be a permanent commitment until the death of one of the spouses, as suggested by Jesus's words in Matthew 19:6–11. While Catholic sacramental marriage is considered to be permanent, it can be annulled under certain conditions. An annulment is not "Catholic divorce" but rather the recognition that the sacramental marriage never took place—either because the rite of matrimony was not celebrated correctly or because one of the parties has not given full consent. Such a determination can only be made by an official Church panel called a marriage tribunal, composed of specially trained priests and laity. Remarriage without an annulment is strictly prohibited according to Catholic doctrine. Catholics who marry Christians from other denominations must receive permission from a bishop.

6. Penance and Reconciliation

In Catholic understanding, Jesus gave His disciples the power to forgive sins. In John 20:23 (NIV), for example, Jesus says to His apostles, "If you forgive anyone's sins, their sins are forgiven; if you do not forgive them, they are not forgiven."

The ability to forgive sins extends to priests, who are understood to be the apostles' successors. The sacrament of penance, now more commonly called the rite of penance and reconciliation, is private and confidential. The confessor enters a special confession room, sits face to face with the priest, says, "Bless me, Father, for I have sinned," and confesses specific sins committed. The priest may ask questions to make sure the confession is thorough, and then he will give "absolution," which is a formula for forgiving the sins. This formula is not automatic; penitents must state—and feel—that they are truly sorry and that they will do their best to not sin again. This is called the act of contrition, and only after this will the priest give the absolution prayer, which is as follows:

> God, the Father of mercies, through the death and resurrection of his Son has reconciled the world to himself and sent the Holy Spirit among us for the forgiveness of sins; through the ministry of the

Church may God give you pardon and peace, and I absolve you from your sins in the name of the Father, and of the Son, and of the Holy Spirit.[5]

The priest then assigns penance, usually in the form of prayers, which the parishioner will need to perform as a necessary part of their reconciliation with God.

7. Extreme Unction

The final sacrament is extreme unction, or anointing of the sick. This sacrament has also been called last rites, but it is not necessarily limited to those on the verge of death. During this sacrament, the priest anoints the sick person with oil by making the sign of the cross on a person's eyes, ears, nostrils, lips, hands, and feet. He says, "Through this holy anointing, and by His most tender mercy, may the Lord pardon you what sins you have committed." If able, the person who has been anointed receives the Eucharist. This is called *viaticum*, a Latin term that originally meant "provisions for a journey." In this case, the journey is to eternal life.

Sacramentals

In addition to the seven sacraments, which form the core of Catholic religious practice worldwide, there are also sacramentals—objects or actions that specially connect people with God. A common sacramental is holy water. As explained, holy water is used by worshippers as they make the sign of the cross (itself a sacramental) as they enter the chapel. Holy water may also be sprinkled on objects to specially bless them. A crucifix, which is an amulet or a statue of Christ crucified, is another sacramental; it makes Catholics mindful of Christ's sacrifice on the cross. Many Catholics wear a crucifix attached to various forms of jewelry.

The rosary is another sacramental distinctively associated with Catholicism. A rosary is a chain of beads that helps guide the wearer through a specific meditation or prayer. The beginning of a rosary is marked by a crucifix, an initial bead, a separation, and then three beads. After this initial chain of beads, there are five groups of ten beads—each called a

---

5. *Catechism of the Catholic Church*, 2nd ed. (Vatican City: Vatican Press, 1997), 364.

decade—separated by a single bead. Reciting the rosary is a common form of prayer and meditation throughout Catholicism. The beads represent prayers: the single bead that begins the rosary, and each bead that marks the gaps between the other five decades, is for saying the Lord's Prayer. The initial three beads and beads in each of the five decades mark recitations of the Hail Mary.[6] At the beginning of each decade of beads, the person reciting the rosary recalls aspects or "mysteries" of the lives of Jesus and Mary. Many Catholics try to carry a rosary with them at all times.

Holy Days of Obligation

In addition to weekly Mass on Sundays, Catholics are formally required to attend Mass on a number of holy days of obligation. The foremost days of obligation are the three days associated with Easter, which together are called the triduum. Because these days occur during the paschal full moon, which is the first full moon after the spring equinox, their timing varies from year to year. The first part of the triduum is Holy Thursday, during which the Last Supper is commemorated. Central to this Mass is the priest washing the feet of twelve congregants in memory of Christ washing the feet of His disciples. Then there is Good Friday, when Jesus's crucifixion is remembered through a series of detailed readings from the Psalms and the Gospels. Finally, there is the celebration of the resurrection of Jesus on Easter Sunday. Preceding Easter is Lent, which is a forty-day period of fasting in preparation for the celebration of Jesus's resurrection. The forty days of Lent begin with a service on Ash Wednesday, when the priest makes the sign of the cross with ashes on the worshipper's forehead and says, "Remember that you are dust and unto dust you shall return." Christmas is also a holy day of obligation, celebrating the birth of Jesus Christ and preceded by a four-week preparatory period called Advent.

Inculturation

Catholicism has a rich and complex history throughout many cultures. Because of this, many Catholic religious practices have a culturally distinct shape and texture depending on local traditions. There have been fierce

---

6. A prayer expressing praise for and asking help of the Virgin Mary.

debates throughout history on how far and to what degree Catholicism can adapt to local cultures. An important example of such a debate was the Chinese rites controversy in the seventeenth and eighteenth centuries. At issue was whether Mandarin Chinese converts could continue to practice Confucian and ancestral rites. Initially, the Vatican suppressed these adaptations. However, more than a hundred years later, they were reexamined and permitted, the reason being that these Chinese customs were considered to be social, rather than religious, in nature.

Observing Catholicism worldwide, one also sees numerous feasts or celebrations dedicated to local saints. One particularly popular feast day in the United States is St. Joseph's Day, which honors Mary's husband. Altars are built to honor St. Joseph, and food is distributed to the poor. Throughout the world, there are celebrations of Mary. In many countries, Mary is honored through a procession in which her image or statue is carried through the town or city. In Chile and the Philippines, those in the procession may also dance to honor her. While Catholicism does have a clear sacramental structure, it is important to remember that Catholic religious practices also take on the particular contours and hues of the cultures in which they are situated.

6

Practices Shared by Roman Catholics and Latter-day Saints

By Dr. Alonzo L. Gaskill

Chapter 2 showed that, despite the differences between Catholic and Latter-day Saint *beliefs*, the two faiths have much in common theologically speaking. It is also true that, although the religious *practices* of Roman Catholics might at first appear to be quite different from those of Latter-day Saint Christians, these two traditions have much in common. What follows is only a sampling of the many parallel practices. Because belief and practice are so closely intertwined, this chapter will also emphasize some of the doctrines associated with commonly held practices.

Baptism

In both Catholicism and Latter-day Saint practice, those being baptized—whether as converts or as those who were born into the faith—are baptized in the name of the Godhead or Trinity. In the Church of Jesus Christ, the baptismal prayer is almost identical to the Catholic formula (mentioned by Dr. Schmalz above). In the Doctrine and Covenants, the baptismal formula for Latter-day Saints is offered as follows: "Having been commissioned of Jesus Christ, I baptize you in the name of the Father, and of the Son, and of the Holy Ghost. Amen" (Doctrine and Covenants 20:73). The primary difference between the two almost identical prayers is the addition of stated authority by the Church of Jesus Christ at the beginning of the prayer. In both traditions, the person being baptized enters into a covenant relationship with God. Roman Catholics renew that covenant relationship through the rite of confirmation and through formal penance assigned by a priest; members of the Church of Jesus Christ renew it through partaking the sacrament of the Lord's Supper on a weekly basis and through constant repentance, which is mediated, where necessary, by priesthood leaders.

Hierarchy of Leadership

Unlike the majority of Christian denominations, most of which are Protestant, Roman Catholics and Latter-day Saints have a leadership structure with multiple layers of hierarchy. Roman Catholics are led by a pope, and the Latter-day Saints are led by a prophet. Catholics have cardinals serving under the pope, while Latter-day Saints have apostles under the prophet. In the Roman Catholic tradition, there are archbishops[1] who have a scope of influence and authority similar to General Authority Seventies in the Church of Jesus Christ. In Catholicism, bishops are roughly equivalent to Latter-day Saint stake presidents, each presiding over numerous congregations within their jurisdiction. Roman Catholics have priests presiding over individual parishes. In the Church of Jesus Christ, bishops preside over wards.

Though the terminology is unique in the two faith traditions, the authority and jurisdiction of the various offices are largely analogous. More importantly, the perception of leadership and revelation in both traditions tends to be fairly "top-down." In other words, Catholics and Latter-day Saints typically hold that revelation for the whole Church comes from the leaders at the highest levels. While local members in both faiths can receive personal impressions and inspiration for their own lives, each denomination tends to see local leaders as having a special right to revelation for their congregation and the general leaders the right to revelation for the Church as a whole.

---

1. A bishop of the highest rank, who is responsible for the bishops within his archdiocese (a larger geographical area encompassing many dioceses).

In this way, Catholics and Latter-day Saints are very much alike—and very different from their Protestant brothers and sisters. The approach to authority influences the practice of Catholics and Latter-day Saints, in that their degree of obedience to papal or prophetic utterance is determined by the degree to which they perceive their leaders as inspired, both in their appointment of other leaders and in their teachings or directives. While certainly members of both traditions struggle to accept top-down leadership, the majority of the members of both faiths embrace this belief, which dramatically influences their personal practices. They perceive their leaders as inspired of God and are willing to comply with counsel and declarations.

In Roman Catholicism, a bishop is selected by the Vatican, and the pope must give final approval of a bishop's selection and ordination. Similarly, Church officials in Salt Lake City review the names of potential bishops, while the president of the Church must give final approval of a bishop's call and ordination. In both traditions, that ordination takes place by the laying on of hands. Even though the jurisdiction of a bishop is different among Catholics and Latter-day Saints, it is significant that in both traditions, God is concerned not only about inspired leadership at the Churchwide level, but it is also understood that He appoints, through inspiration and priesthood authority, leaders at *all* levels.

Views on Marriage and Family

As societal trends continue to influence the beliefs and practices of Catholics and Latter-day Saints, the leaders of both of these churches have generally held conservative views on marriage and the family. In Catholic and Latter-day Saint doctrine, marriage is specifically defined as being between one man and one woman, and immorality of any kind has been repeatedly condemned by the leadership of these two faiths. To be in good standing and worthy to participate in the sacraments or ordinances of either tradition, one is expected to live a morally upright life. In addition, the leaders of both Roman Catholics and Latter-day Saints have expressed concern regarding the breakdown of the family and the consequences that has on faith, the well-being of individuals, and civilization itself.

In practice, therefore, Catholics and Latter-day Saints have come together in defense of traditional marriage and the family. Both traditions have been harshly criticized for taking traditional positions on such matters, particularly in an era of shifting morality and evolving views of the family. Additionally, both traditions declare that their position on morality and family life comes from a divine source—be it scripture or modern revelation—and thus constitutes God's will for the world.

Saving Ordinances

Both traditions have sacramental rites or ordinances that influence the salvation of the member. Catholics have baptism, as do Latter-day Saints. (Both also have confirmation, but the ordinance is different in the two denominations.) Each has the sacrament of the Lord's Supper. Each has penance and reconciliation, or formal repentance. Both Catholics and Latter-day Saints anoint the sick with consecrated oil. Both have rites of ordination. And the two traditions see marriage as sacramental.

The sacraments or sacred rites of the Church are central to the life and practice of an active Catholic or Latter-day Saint. In both traditions, the faithful attend church regularly and partake of the sacrament of the Lord's Supper often. In both faiths, the practice of daily repentance is seen as imperative. Each sees its clergy as helpful in the laity's pursuit of salvation and beneficial to their spiritual wellbeing here in mortality. A Church-sanctioned marriage (performed by a priest or sealer) is the goal, as a sacramental marriage performed under the Church's unique authority is seen in both traditions as being accepted by God in ways exceeding a secular union. Thus, for both faiths, the practice of a sacrament-filled life is emphasized as a means of accessing God's saving grace.

Sacramentals and Rituals

In addition to sacraments, each Church has sacramentals, though only Catholics use the term. These behaviors or objects are attached to ordinances or sacraments and thus have a sacred place in religious practices. For example, Catholics use holy water, while Latter-day Saints use consecrated olive oil. In the Catholic Church, liturgical clothing is commonly worn, and in Latter-day Saint temples, temple garments and other articles of ceremonial clothing are an important feature. Whereas Catholics might use statues of the Virgin Mary in or on their churches, statues of the angel Moroni are common on Latter-day Saint temples and elsewhere. The sacramentals of both traditions help practitioners to connect with God. For both traditions, these symbols remind the faithful of God, His plan, their obligations to Him, and how His power can bless and sanctify their lives.

One other element associated with religious practice is the local flavor found in the two respective religions. While both faiths have components of their tradition that are consistent throughout the world, practices in both are also affected by the local culture and leadership, depending on where the religion is practiced. For example, in the Church of Jesus Christ, specific hymns are sung more often than others in certain parts of the world. And in England, the sacrament table is often set up differently than in the United States. In the Roman Catholic tradition, the Mass can look quite different from country to country, or congregation to congregation. The way the hymns are sung, the architecture, and the vestments of the priests can differ among countries and cultures. There can be quite a bit of variety in the supplementary practice of each tradition. The essentials, however, are uniform.

7

Differences between Latter-day Saint and Roman Catholic Practices

By Dr. Alonzo L. Gaskill

Baptism

Most Latter-day Saints are familiar with one way their faith differs from Catholicism: Catholics are typically baptized in their infancy, whereas members of the Church of Jesus Christ are usually baptized at about eight years of age—when they become "accountable," according to Church doctrine (see Doctrine and Covenants 20:71; Doctrine and Covenants 68:27). Both faiths understand the Bible as commanding baptism (see John 3:5), but they differ on the application of the commandment. In an effort to fulfill this commandment as early as possible, Catholics baptize newborns. Members of the Church of Jesus Christ, on the other hand, wait until a child appears old enough to understand and embrace the ordinance because it is believed that accountability requires understanding. Because of the Church of Jesus Christ's belief in vicarious work for the dead, they do not share the traditional Roman Catholic concern for those who have died unbaptized. The timing of Catholic baptism correlates directly with the belief in original sin, and Latter-day Saint practice correlates with the belief that all are born without sin and remain so until they are old enough to understand the spiritual implications of their actions and thoughts (see Moses 6:53–60).

The mode of baptism in Roman Catholicism is also different from that performed in the restored gospel. Latter-day Saints baptize by immersion, whereas Catholics typically do not. Instead of immersion, Catholics will typically baptize by affusion, or pouring. In addition, Latter-day Saints make covenants when they are baptized, while it is common for Catholic babies being baptized to have one or more godparents (and traditionally their biological parents) make the vows on behalf of the child. Years later, when children are old enough to take those vows upon themselves, they participate in a confirmation ceremony, wherein they "confirm" what was promised on their behalf at their infant baptism, which they now are able to make for themselves because of their age, accountability, and spiritual maturity.

Priesthood Ordination

In the Church of Jesus Christ, as in Catholicism, the choice to pursue priesthood ordination is a personal one. However, in the Catholic Church, ordination requires many years of academic training first, whereas in the restored gospel, one's academic background is seen as irrelevant to one's qualification to be ordained.

In order to be ordained a priest in the Catholic Church, a man must not only be living a morally upright life and express belief in the faith, but he must also in most cases earn a bachelor's degree and then attend seminary for many years, earning a master's degree or the equivalent. In the Church of Jesus Christ, by contrast, there are no educational prerequisites to ordination; one must reach the minimum age associated with a priesthood office, be living a morally upright life, and profess a belief in the Church's major tenets. While Catholicism stresses that men should pursue priesthood ordination only if they first feel a "call from God," in the Church of Jesus Christ, young men tend to be ordained and advance in the priesthood almost automatically during the year that they turn twelve, fourteen, sixteen, and eighteen. They are interviewed for worthiness, belief, and a desire to be ordained, but there is not a significant emphasis on a young man feeling a "call from God" to be ordained to the priesthood.

Church Leadership

In Catholicism, becoming a parish priest (or leader of a congregation) is something one chooses for one's self, based on a sense of being called by God to serve in that capacity. Not all priestly vocations or jobs in Catholicism are associated with working with a congregation, and priests select an order of the priesthood they pursue based on what priestly job they feel called to do or are interested in doing. While in the Catholic model a man chooses to preside over a congregation because he feels a call to do so, in the Church of Jesus Christ one does not choose to become a bishop over a local congregation—one is called by the president of the Church and invited by the stake president to accept that assignment. It is a volunteer position, not a vocation.

In Catholicism, the role of a priest is a lifelong vocation, whereas the Church of Jesus Christ calls, ordains, and sets a man apart to serve as a bishop for only a handful of years, and then he is released from that assignment and someone else is called to replace him. The Latter-day Saint bishop still holds the priesthood office of bishop once released just as a Catholic priest remains a priest the rest of his life, but in general, Latter-day Saints actively serve in the role for only about five years. Priests in the Catholic tradition are expected to be single and celibate; bishops in the Church of Jesus Christ are married or widowed.

Sacrament of the Lord's Supper

Many Roman Catholics partake of the sacrament of the Lord's Supper each week, and some remarkably devout members partake daily. Formally speaking, however, it is only requisite that one participate in that sacrament at Easter. In the Church of Jesus Christ, the sacrament of the Lord's Supper is tied to forgiveness of sins and the renewal of covenants, so active members are encouraged to partake of this ordinance each week. Traditionally, many Roman Catholics go to confession once a week, as that sacrament is tied to repentance in their faith. Latter-day Saints, on the other hand, are encouraged to repent each day, and involving local priesthood authorities in one's repentance process is typically reserved for serious sins. Members of the Church of Jesus Christ, then, use the sacrament of the Lord's Supper much like Catholics use their sacrament of penance—seeking forgiveness for the sins of the last week.

Marriage

Roman Catholics typically perceive marriages performed in the Church as lasting until the death of one of the spouses. The rite is seen as sacramental, but it is not seen as forging an eternal relationship between the husband and wife. In the Church of Jesus Christ, however, the ordinance or sacrament of marriage is seen as making an eternal covenant. In both traditions, a sacramental marriage (that is, a Church marriage for Catholics and a temple marriage for Latter-day Saints) is viewed as higher than being married by a civil authority. Nonetheless, there is no formal doctrine of eternal marriage or eternal families in the Roman Catholic tradition. Thus, while some Catholics assume they will recognize their mortal spouse or children in heaven, they do not expect to be married in the next life or to have a family relationship in the eternities.

Additionally, in Catholicism, marriage is not required for salvation. A person who goes through life single and celibate has the same opportunity to get to heaven as the married person. Indeed, some Catholics would perceive the single celibate as more likely to make it to heaven than the married Catholic. Contrast that with the Latter-day Saint belief that in order to receive the highest degree of the celestial kingdom—in order to be exalted—one is obligated (whether her or in the hereafter) to be married and sealed to one's spouse, and then keep the covenants associated with that sacred ordinance.

Repentance

The act or sacrament of repentance is fundamental to both Latter-day Saints and Catholics, yet they understand and practice repentance differently. In Catholicism, priests have the power to forgive sins and absolve the sinner. This practice is based on the idea that priests act in the stead of Christ—in His place, as His earthly representatives. In the Church of Jesus Christ, on the other hand, the presiding high priest (that is, the bishop or stake president) does not have the power to forgive or absolve sin, only to guide a penitent person through the repentance process.

In the Roman Catholic tradition, repentance is more than a mental process. It is in many ways a rite, laden with formally established prayers and behaviors. Thus, when one participates in confession, one's "confessor" (the priest or bishop) discusses the sins committed and then instructs the penitent regarding what things will be required in order to resolve the sinful acts. The assigned penance typically involves reciting a certain number of prayers such as the Lord's Prayer or the Hail Mary. For more serious sins, more serious penance would likely be required, and a longer period of penance might be expected.

Compare that to common Latter-day Saint practice, in which the repentant sinner daily asks for God's forgiveness through prayer, sometimes coupled with fasting or other signs of contrition. She or he asks for Christ's enabling power to overcome and forsake sinful thoughts, desires, or behaviors. A priesthood leader's mediation is not seen as necessary for typical day-to-day failings, though partaking of the sacrament of the Lord's Supper is seen as a necessary part of addressing one's daily sins.

When a Latter-day Saint has committed what might be seen as a serious transgression, however—something that might put one's membership or full fellowship in jeopardy—he or she would need to confess that transgression to the stake president or bishop. Like Catholics, Latter-day Saint Christians perceive their priesthood leader as an earthly representative of Christ and a "common judge in Israel." Nevertheless, they do not perceive Christ as having divinely invested their leaders with the specific authority to forgive or absolve sins. Rather, bishops and stake presidents are understood to receive the "mantle" of authority that allows them to sense what Jesus would require of someone seeking His forgiveness. That mantle or position also endows the Latter-day Saint bishop or stake president with a gift of discernment, enabling him to know when the repentant person has completed the repentance process. Thus, while a stake president or bishop has a role to play in helping Church members repent, it is Christ who forgives, through His Atonement.

The repentance process in the Church of Jesus Christ feels somewhat similar to Catholicism in that it employs rules, processes, and acts of penance as a means of repenting of serious sins. However, for Latter-day Saints the process of repenting of most sins is individual, and forgiveness is seen as coming through mental, emotional, and spiritual exercises—personal prayers, partaking of the sacrament, and seeking to change one's thoughts and actions—with limited or no guidance from a mortal mediator.

8

Common Misperceptions of Catholicism

By Dr. Mathew N. Schmalz

Latter-day Saints and Catholics share the experience of having to confront misconceptions and prejudices concerning their respective religious beliefs and rituals. As far as Catholicism is concerned, most misperceptions arise in three general areas: the pope, Mary, and the saints, and the sacraments.

The Pope

The first time I attended a Protestant service, I was staying over for the weekend at my best friend's house. I was in sixth grade and didn't realize that religion was a subject often avoided in polite conversation. After attending a Methodist service, I asked my friend's mother why Protestants didn't believe in the pope. "Shouldn't Jesus be head of the Church?" was the response I received.

For Catholics, the pope is the chief teaching authority and administrative head for the institutional Church on earth. But the Church is not simply an earthly reality; it is a supernatural and heavenly one as well. Catholicism has a number of metaphors for understanding Jesus as ultimate head of the Church, such as referring to the Church as "the body" or "bride of Christ."

Each metaphor affirms that Jesus is intimately united with the Church. No Catholic that I know would deny that Jesus is the head of the Church in its earthly and spiritual totality.

Mary and the Saints

Catholicism believes that Mary and the saints are intercessors or advocates for our personal prayers, as well as models for us in life. Many Catholics have a prayerful relationship both with Mary and with an individual saint who is called a "patron saint."[1] For example, I have two saints that are part of my prayer life: St. Thomas, the apostle to India; and St. Jude, the patron of hopeless causes.

One of the main criticisms of Catholic religious life and practice is that Catholics actually worship Mary and the saints on the same level of God Himself. But Catholics do not worship Mary or the saints at all. The Latin word *dulia* refers to the reverence or veneration given to the saints as exemplary models of Christian life. *Dulia* is less than the *hyperdulia,* or intensive veneration, offered to Mary. But the respect offered to Mary is always considered to be less than the worship owed to the Trinity. *Latria,* again a word from Latin, refers to the worship that is directed to the Creator alone.

Of course, not all Catholics are aware of the theological distinctions between *dulia, hyperdulia,* and *latria.* But Catholics are generally aware of the distinction between veneration—understood as giving reverence to someone—and worship. In the end, all worship and prayer is understood to be fundamentally offered to God.

Sacraments

When I look at how Catholicism in depicted in film, it strikes me how often the sacrament of reconciliation is portrayed as a kind of "get out of jail free" card: you just have to confess your sins and then your slate is cleaned—you can go on sinning as long as you keep repeating the process. But this is certainly not what confession is, or should be, according to Catholic understanding. An effective and valid confession has three parts: experiencing sorrow for one's sins (contrition), admitting specific sins to a priest

---

1. A saint who is a special advocate of a particular cause, place, occupation, or person.

(confession), and showing a willingness to change one's behavior (repentance). Priests can deny absolution if any one of these elements is not present. Therefore, someone who goes to confession with no intent of amending her or his ways is not abiding by the intent and spirit of this important Catholic sacrament.

Perhaps the sacrament that is most frequently misunderstood is the Eucharist. To review: Eucharist means "thanksgiving" in Greek and refers to the celebration of the Mass, in which the sacrament of bread and wine becomes the body and blood of Jesus Christ. I have had people tell me that the whole idea was strange or hard to understand. People have even told me that Catholics essentially practice cannibalism. So, some further explanation is usually in order.

As previously explained, transubstantiation is the theological concept that is most helpful to understanding how bread and wine become the real body and blood of Christ. According to transubstantiation, only the external appearances of bread and wine remain; the inner reality is permanently changed to the body and blood of Jesus Christ. So, it is true that the presence of Jesus's body and blood in the bread and wine is not symbolic: it is real and actual. However, we are not talking about the physical presence of Jesus as a figure from history. Instead, Jesus is present sacramentally—something that is hard to explain fully without referring to complex Catholic discussions initiated when theologians attempted to integrate the Greek philosophy (particularly the work of Aristotle) into Catholic thinking. While it is finally one of the deepest mysteries of the Catholic faith, the sacramental presence of Jesus is most appropriately understood as a metaphysical assertion, which affirms that the body, blood, soul and divinity of Jesus Christ are together really and substantially present under the appearance of bread and wine. This is why it is called Communion. It is a special way Catholics can intensify their closeness to Christ.

9

Appreciation for Roman Catholic Religious Practices

By Dr. Alonzo L. Gaskill

As described in this work, Catholicism is rich with traditions from which Latter-day Saint Christians might learn. The unique ways in which Catholics worship—the ways their religious lives are steeped in devotion and symbolism—can inspire a sense of appreciation. This chapter addresses only two such practices.

Sunday Liturgy

Latter-day Saints are not accustomed to speaking of Church liturgy, but they are generally familiar with the idea it expresses—the set of practices and rituals that constitute public worship. The Sunday liturgy of the Church of Jesus Christ contrasts significantly with the liturgy found in temple worship. In Latter-day Saint tradition, Sabbath services are simple in nature (sometimes called low liturgy) and temple ordinances and performances have deep symbolic significance (high liturgy). Whereas the Roman Catholic Church's high liturgy of the Mass contrasts with the low liturgy of the Latter-day Saint Sunday sacrament services, Catholic Sunday liturgy is more comparable to the high liturgy of Latter-day Saint temples.

Because of the contrast between Catholic and Latter-day Saint services, members of the Church of Jesus Christ may experience an appreciation for the sensitivity and meaning Roman Catholics find in symbolism. Catholics are saturated in symbols from early in their lives, so they tend to relate well to symbolism and high liturgies. Consequentially, members of the Church of Jesus Christ may learn from the Catholic tradition of developing symbolic literacy at a young age, and this in turn might help them learn from the temple experience, other ordinances, and even the scriptures.

Art and Architecture

On a related note, early Catholic churches were designed as teaching devices. For many centuries, Church members were often illiterate and Catholic services were presented in Latin, a language they did not know. Therefore, one way for them to learn the Bible and Christian history was through visual depictions of these sacred stories in the art and architecture of the church buildings. The Catholic Church's artwork was designed as a means of conveying stories and teaching doctrines. As is well known, stained glass windows were not simply for the purpose of beautifying a building—though they do that well. Rather, the windows of the churches and cathedrals of Catholicism told the foundational stories of the faith and enabled those who could not read or did not have access to the sacred texts a way to learn and remember some of the most important narratives of Christianity.

Other pieces of art, such as paintings and statues, and even the layout and architecture of the buildings, served as teaching devices that had significance in times past and, when understood, have symbolic value today. When compared to Roman Catholic churches, the Latter-day Saints' Sunday meetinghouses are bare and utilitarian. The vast majority of the chapels of the Church of Jesus Christ are functional in their design but not in and of themselves intended as teaching tools. Though some artwork is found in the foyers and offices of the Latter-day Saint chapels, when compared to a typical Roman Catholic church, Latter-day Saint meetinghouses look almost Quaker in their inner appearance and simplicity.

Latter-day Saint temples are a different matter altogether. Aside from the spirit present in those sacred edifices and the holy work performed there, one thing that often draws the Saints to their temples is their love for the grandeur and splendor of the architecture and art. The peace and beauty of the celestial room, for example, is almost unparalleled. Endowed Latter-day Saints are drawn there, as they contemplate what heaven will be like.

While The Church of Jesus Christ of Latter-day Saints seeks to create a Sunday worship experience that is free from distractions (hence the lack of art in their chapels), there may be something to be learned from the Catholic experience which, in a way, reflects the temple experience of members of the Church of Jesus Christ. Art and architecture can be spiritually inspiring and can invoke the Holy Spirit. The Church of Jesus Christ buildings will likely not start featuring grand works of art, yet incorporating religious art may benefit and inspire Church members in their worship experience, drawing them to Christ. Contemplating visual art can help Latter-day Saints have a more Spirit-filled experience with the sacrament and the Sabbath.

SECTION 3
Interfaith Dialogue

This final section begins with a brief survey of how members of the Church of Jesus Christ have viewed and interacted with Catholics from the 1830s to the present day. It then introduces principles for good interfaith dialogue, both generally and in Latter-day Saint–Catholic interactions specifically. Finally, it presents thoughts on the beauty of Latter-day Saint doctrine and practice from a Catholic perspective.

10

Latter-day Saint Engagement with Roman Catholicism

By Dr. Alonzo L. Gaskill

The relationship between Roman Catholics and members of the Church of Jesus Christ has at times been rocky. Although today most would presume that the two traditions generally get along well and have a mutual respect for each other's contributions to the world and to Christianity, their relationship to each other has had its ups and downs.

After a March 2019 meeting with Pope Francis, President Russell M. Nelson noted, "The differences in doctrine [between our two churches] are real. They are important. But they are not nearly as important as things we have in common—our concern for human suffering, our desire for and the importance of religious liberty for all of society, and the importance of building bridges of friendship instead of building walls of segregation."[1] While the Church of Jesus Christ's official views on Catholicism and its important contributions are positive, some Latter-day Saint Christians continue to hold

---

1. Sarah Jane Weaver, "President Nelson Meets with Pope Francis at the Vatican," *Church News*, 9 Mar. 2019, https://www.churchofjesuschrist.org/church/news/president-nelson-meets-with-pope-francis-at-the-vatican.

more negative opinions regarding Catholicism. A brief review of some of the history may prove helpful in explaining why.

Historical Latter-day Saint Views of Catholicism

From early in their history, many members of the Church of Jesus Christ held strongly negative feelings about Roman Catholicism. Initially, Latter-day Saints tended to view Catholics through the lenses of nineteenth-century Protestantism, which was bitter and critical of the Roman Catholic Church.

Most Protestants before and during Joseph Smith's time saw Roman Catholicism as the figure described in Revelation 17:5: "Babylon the Great, the Mother of Harlots and Abominations of the Earth." Following this lead, some early members of the Church of Jesus Christ often spoke of Catholicism as the "great and abominable church." The various Protestant denominations, meanwhile, were sometimes considered by early Saints as the "offspring" or "daughters" of the "great harlot."

In the Book of Mormon, Nephi's description of "that abominable church" was often perceived as a reference to the Catholic Church—particularly because of language such as 1 Nephi 13:8: "Behold the gold [of the great and abominable church], and the silver, and the silks, and the scarlets, and the fine-twined linen, and the precious clothing." For most members of the Church of Jesus Christ, this sounded very much like the liturgical elements of the Roman Catholic tradition. First Nephi 14:10 states, "Behold there are save two churches only; the one is the church of the Lamb of God, and the other is the church of the devil; wherefore, whoso belongeth not to the church of the Lamb of God belongeth to that great church, which is the mother of abominations; and she is the whore of all the earth." Some early Latter-day Saints saw themselves as "the church of the Lamb of God," and, thus, the Roman Catholics could only be "the church of the devil."

This association of Catholics with the "church of the devil" remained in the discourse of certain leaders of the Church until at least 1958, when Elder Bruce R. McConkie (then a member of the First Council of the Seventy) published the first edition of his book *Mormon Doctrine*. However, since the entries explicitly critical of the Catholic Church were removed from the 1966 revised edition of that popular text, much of the anti-Catholic rhetoric has faded, particularly among General Authorities—though some Latter-day Saint members continue to presume that the "true identity" of the great and abominable church is Roman Catholicism.

Adding to the anti-Catholic sentiment common among some Latter-day Saint Christians was the reality that Protestants converted to the Church of Jesus Christ at a much higher rate in the late nineteenth and early twentieth century than did Catholics, who at that time were largely unreceptive to the message of the Restoration. For some, this only solidified their belief that the devil was in the details of Catholicism.

Times of Unity

Of course, not everything regarding interactions between Catholics and Latter-day Saints has been negative. Indeed, some leaders and members of the Church of Jesus Christ have long sought to build bridges and defend Catholics when it was evident they were being discriminated against. For example, in 1835, Oliver Cowdery publicly expressed concern about the torching of a Roman Catholic convent in Boston, noting that the persecution against Catholics in the United States was "shameful."[2] Brigham Young is said to have helped out Father Edward Kelly when Kelly was involved in a land dispute regarding the title to a Catholic church property in Salt Lake City.[3]

In the 1950s, when the Catholics were desperate for a place to hold Mass in La Sal, in Utah's San Juan County, Latter-day Saint philanthropist Charles Hardy Redd Sr. initially offered to let them use a vacant bunkhouse he owned. Then, Redd donated to the Catholic Church the land where the Sacred Heart Mission church building would be built.[4] Decades before in St. George, Utah, a Latter-day Saint choir director named John M. MacFarlane offered to let Bishop Lawrence J. Scanlan celebrate Mass in the newly completed St. George tabernacle—and McFarlane's St. George Tabernacle Choir provided the music. Bishop Scanlan was even invited to publish a lengthy description of Catholic beliefs in the first issue of one of the Church's periodicals, *The Improvement Era*.[5]

---

2. *Latter-day Saints Messenger and Advocate*, Oct. 1836, 3:393.
3. See Bernice Maher Mooney and Msgr. Jerome C. Stoffel, *Salt of the Earth: The History of the Catholic Diocese of Salt Lake City, 1776--987* (Salt Lake City, UT: The Catholic Diocese of Salt Lake City, 1987), 41.
4. See Mooney and Stoffel (1987), 272.
5. Rev. Lawrence Scanlon, "The Doctrine and Claims of the Roman Catholic Church," *Improvement Era*, Nov. 1897, 1:11–25.

Throughout the comparatively short history of The Church of Jesus Christ of Latter-day Saints, some Catholics have also spoken up on behalf of their Latter-day Saint brothers and sisters, particularly during the federal efforts to dissolve the Church of Jesus Christ over concern about plural marriage in the late nineteenth century. Owing to their history of persecution by Protestants in the United States, Catholics could see for themselves that, should federal attacks on the Church of Jesus Christ succeed, Catholics might well become the next victims of government-sanctioned intolerance. Additionally, current Roman Catholic scholars like Stephen Webb have written in defense of Latter-day Saints as Christians, arguing that, though their brand of Christianity is "exotic," many Christians fail "to realize just how deeply Christ-centered Mormonism is."[6]

In recent times, the two faiths have frequently worked hand in hand on various projects, including political and social issues—particularly those concerning religious freedom, the protection of the family, and the sanctity of marriage. In the last couple of decades, Catholic and Latter-day Saint relief organizations have consistently worked together to respond to natural disasters in various parts of the world. In the twenty-first century, hostility has largely faded, and the two faith traditions seem much more inclined to forget the past and instead seek for a working relationship moving into the future.

---

6. Stephen H. Webb, *Mormon Christianity: What Other Christians Can Learn From the Latter-day Saints* (New York: Oxford University Press, 2013), 114–115.

11

Best Practices for Interfaith Dialogue with Roman Catholics

By Dr. Alonzo L. Gaskill

The primary purpose of interfaith dialogue should always be understanding and bridge-building, never debate or argument. When the focus of a discussion becomes proving who is right or who is wrong, the discussion has officially become unproductive. Thus, in their interactions with other faith communities, members of The Church of Jesus Christ of Latter-day Saints should seek to enlighten and understand, not to debate. The Lord Himself has cautioned us: "Contention is not of me, but is of the devil, who is the father of contention, and he stirreth up the hearts of men to contend with anger, one with another" (3 Nephi 11:29).

There are principles of good interfaith dialogue which are generally applicable, and others more specific to interactions with Roman Catholics. We will consider both in this chapter, starting with general principles.

General Principles for Interfaith Dialogue

Krister Stendahl, former bishop in the Church of Sweden and past dean of the Harvard Divinity School, offered what he called "three rules of religious understanding." These commonly cited rules are first, when seeking to try to understand the beliefs and practices of another religious tradition, one should ask practitioners of that tradition about their faith, rather than asking an enemy of that faith tradition. Second, one should always avoid comparing one's own religion's best to another religion's worst. Rather, compare best to best—so as to be fair, and so as to see the other tradition in a positive and accurate light. Third, Stendhal recommended that one always "leave room for holy envy"; in other words, when looking at another faith tradition, we should be open to recognizing and highlighting parts of that tradition that we find inspiring.[1]

Another principle of good interfaith dialogue, which Latter-day Saint Christians would be wise to practice, has to do with the query "Why?" Believe it or not, "Why?" can be a loaded question. When you ask someone why they do or believe something, you may sound as though you are suggesting they should not believe or practice what you are inquiring about. There is little room for a positive way to take such questions. However, if you instead ask "What?" or "How?" questions (such as "What in your tradition helps you to feel closest to God?" or "How do you use scripture in your tradition?"), you will most likely sound less like you are criticizing their beliefs or practices. If you must ask a "Why?" question, it is often best to preface it with a positive affirmation, such as "I've always been so impressed by the reverence you show for the sacrament of the Lord's Supper. Would you please tell me more about why you do that?" The positive affirmation as a preface to your question will help the person of another faith know that you respect their religious beliefs and practices, and that you are not challenging it but are genuinely trying to understand it. As a Roman Catholic friend of mine recently said to me, "Asking Catholics *why* they do things is a good way to make them run for the door!"

It is also wise to avoid media sensationalism. Odds are, if you are getting your information about another religion from something you saw on TV, or in a tabloid, it is skewed, inaccurate, or offensive—or all of the above. Of all people, Latter-day Saints should relate to that fact! If a controversy about a

---

1. These "Three Rules of Religious Understanding" were presented by Stendahl at a press conference in Stockholm, Sweden, on November 23, 1987, where he responded to rather vocal opposition to the fact that The Church of Jesus Christ of Latter-day Saints had built a temple in Stockholm. One source noted that, through Stendahl's op eds and other public statements in support of the Church, he was "instrumental in the temple being built" in Sweden. See Barnard N. Madsen, *The Truman G. Madsen Story: A Life of Study and Faith* (Salt Lake City, UT: Deseret Book, 2016), 361. See Madsen (2016), 367, for a summarization of Stendahl's "three rules for religious understanding."

given religious tradition is playing out in the media, it is best not to approach a practitioner of the faith currently being "dragged through the mud" and ask them about how they feel about what is being said about them in the news. No matter how curious you are, it is always best to avoid stepping on already bruised toes. One should not ask a member of The Church of Jesus Christ of Latter-day Saints, "How many wives do you have?" One shouldn't ask a Muslim, "How do you feel about terrorism?" And one should not ask a Roman Catholic, "How do you feel about the recent scandals associated with your clergy?" If your question will likely cause the person you're asking to think, "Oh, here we go again," don't go there.

Another principle of good interfaith dialogue concerns objects that are sacred to other people. Whether it is the crucifix of a Roman Catholic, the icon of an Eastern Orthodox Christian, the yarmulke of a practicing Jew, or the sacred space of a Muslim, Hindu, or Krishna, treat their sacred items and sacred space in the same reverent way you would wish your own sacred items or space be treated. Thus, just as a member of The Church of Jesus Christ of Latter-day Saints would want others to respect the sacred nature of temples and their associated ordinances and clothing, they should respect ordinances and objects associated with other religious traditions.

On a related note, we should never ridicule or make fun of other people's religious beliefs or practices. These represent their sincere faith and genuine desire to connect with God. Even if we do not believe as they do or practice as they do, we should be thrilled at their manifestations of faith in God and their sincere efforts to connect with the divine. We should also remember that some Latter-day Saint beliefs and practices (e.g., temple work for the dead, the wearing of temple garments, or the belief that we can become as God is) also look strange to those not of the faith. Just as we would wish for others to be respectful of these sacred components of our tradition, we should not make light of their beliefs or practices.

Next, when you visit another religious tradition's worship services, engage in a respectful and attentive manner to the degree you feel comfortable. An article in the October 1977 *Ensign* titled "Respect for Other People's Beliefs" counseled members of the Church:

> So far as it does not offend our own religious understanding, we can observe the customs of other people when we are their guests. That means that a Latter-day Saint who enters a Catholic cathedral can take off his hat, if he is a man, or cover her head, if she is a

woman [in places like Latin America]. That means that a shrine that believers approach only after removing their shoes can be shown the same respect by Latter-day Saint visitors. These things show courtesy to the people who believe—no one will suppose that we are worshipping. They will only appreciate our politeness.[2]

When attending the worship service of another religion, you should not partake of nor participate in any of their sacraments. However, generally speaking, if you are going to visit another religion, you should show respect by not being there as a "gawker" but, instead, as one who reverently participates with propriety and respect.

Contention is the opposite of respect. Arguing about religion prevents the presence of the Holy Spirit—and reduces the likelihood that those with whom we argue will feel the Spirit around us or be converted to the ideas we contentiously share. We should not debate or argue about who is right or wrong but seek to listen, understand, appreciate, and share the truths which have meant so much to us in our own lives. The *Ensign* article quoted above also noted:

> We may . . . offend in discussions with our good friends and neighbors, when we only half listen to their half of the conversation, all the time preparing what *we're* going to say when it's *our* turn. . . . Really listening to another's beliefs is hardly a waste of our time, because we very seldom convert with a one-way, me-to-you monologue. Conversion is usually a mixed process of acceptance of some new ideas and rejection of some old ideas—and that takes dialogue. And in order to have honest dialogue, we need to have respect for other people's beliefs for the good that is in them—"them" referring to both the people and their beliefs.

Let us share and explain, listen and learn—rather than simply speaking and correcting our brothers and sisters of other faith traditions.

In addition, it is important to remember that context shapes dialogue. If your sole or primary purpose in having a gospel discussion with someone of a different faith is their conversion to *your* church, they will likely perceive

---

2. Gerald E. Jones, "Respect for Other People's Beliefs," *Ensign*, October 1977, https://www.churchofjesuschrist.org/study/ensign/1977/10/respect-for-other-peoples-beliefs.

that. If, on the other hand, you sincerely want to get to know who they are and what they believe, your conversation and your relationship will be more genuine and long-lasting. There is nothing wrong with wanting someone else to have what has been the greatest blessing to you in your life. However, too often when someone declines to "investigate" the Church, Latter-day Saints pull back and cease to be friends, which clearly sends the message that we were never truly interested in knowing them or having a genuine relationship with them. Our reasons for asking and sharing have to be deeper than simply converting someone. Our actions need to come from a genuine love and interest in understanding another human being.

I had a recurring experience when I was a graduate student in theology at the University of Notre Dame. In that predominately Catholic environment, when people realized that I was a Latter-day Saint Christian, they would often ask me, "Why aren't you at BYU instead of here?" I realized they were not trying to be rude. Nonetheless, it was not the most welcoming thing to say. Occasionally, I felt like an outsider. Dr. Schmalz has commented to me that he knows a number of Roman Catholics living in predominately Latter-day Saint communities who feel oppressed or marginalized because they are in the religious minority. When one is in that situation, there is often what he has called a "perceived power imbalance" that needs to be considered whenever doing dialogue or outreach. For the Latter-day Saint who lives in a predominately homogenized theological community, it is important to remember this dynamic when talking to a friend of another faith. Do all that you can to diminish the imbalance and to help others feel that they are as important to the community as the religious majority is. Help them to see that you value their presence, contributions, and views on life in your community.

In our interactions with members of other religions, it is paramount that we remember that they too are children of their Father in Heaven—and He loves them just as much as He loves you and me. We too should feel a sincere and deep love for them. We should value them, see the good in them, and earnestly strive to understand what they believe, why they believe it, and how it helps them to connect with God. The Prophet Joseph Smith taught, "Love is one of the leading characteristics of Deity, and ou[gh]t to be manifested by those who aspire to be the Sons of God."[3] Members of The Church of Jesus

---

3. Joseph Smith to Quorum of the Twelve, 15 Dec. 1840, https://www.josephsmithpapers.org/paper-summary/letter-to-quorum-of-the-twelve-15-december-1840/2.

Christ of Latter-day Saints believe that they have the "fulness of the gospel" and additional truths that others have lost or do not have access to. If a "fulness" of the doctrine of divine love is not one of those truths we firmly hold to, then how is our faith really a benefit to us or the world? This love will allow the Spirit to be present in our interactions and will enable us to develop more of the attributes of Christ in our own lives, as we seek to love, bless, serve, and understand people who do not share our beliefs.

Principles for Interfaith Dialogue with Catholics

In addition to the previous general recommendations, I would like to add six principles or practices that can help guide Latter-day Saints in their interactions, particularly with Roman Catholics. These ideas can lead to better relationships and better understanding, facilitating respect on both sides.

First, because the Church of Jesus Christ strives for uniformity in doctrine, practice, and administration, members of the Church often wrongly assume that other religions work that same way. In fact, most religions, Christian or otherwise, are not nearly as concerned about the doctrinal orthodoxy of their members. Prior to the Second Vatican Council in the 1960s (often referred to as Vatican II), Roman Catholics emphasized uniformity much more than they do now. Today, Catholics are diverse in belief and practice. One can be a Catholic in good standing with the Church and openly disagree with the Church's official teachings, or not be supportive of the pope, or not participate in the religious life of the Church. Latter-day Saint Christians need to remember when they interact with a member of the Catholic Church that not everyone approves of every official doctrine or traditional view associated with Catholicism. This is one more reason to get to know your Catholic neighbor, as Catholicism varies from nation to nation, parish to parish, and family to family.

The second principle is related to Krister Stendahl's suggestion that if you want to know about a particular religion's beliefs or practices, ask an active practitioner of that faith rather than someone antagonistic to that faith tradition. When it comes to Roman Catholicism, there is one additional facet to that advice. As a Catholic friend of mine pointed out, since Roman Catholicism is quite hierarchical, it is often best to talk to the priest first if you have questions about theology or practice. That is not to suggest that you should not engage in dialogue with your practicing Catholic neighbor. It is important to remember, though, that Catholics do not always understand their theology in the same way as Church officials. Thus, some Catholics might feel a little uncomfortable being asked detailed theological questions by someone outside their faith tradition and would rather accompany you on a visit to their parish priest to ask about their faith, rather than answer the questions themselves.

Third, in the long history of Catholicism, there were periods of forced conversion and adherence to the faith—practices that thankfully do not at all resemble what goes on in the Catholic Church today. In fact, many Catholics do not think of their faith as ever being aggressive in its proselyting, but they often see members of The Church of Jesus Christ of Latter-day Saints as exactly that—aggressive proselytizers. And they may be right! Religions that are more actively engaged in evangelizing (or proselyting) those of other faith traditions are often more comfortable with Latter-day Saint missionary techniques. Since evangelizing is less common among lay Catholics today, sometimes they are put off by those who are seem overly enthusiastic about their missionary efforts. For Roman Catholics as much as anyone, a "full-court press" to make a convert may not be well received.

A fourth best practice when engaging in interfaith dialogue with Roman Catholics has to do with the tendency, discussed in the previous chapter, of some Latter-day Saints to see the Roman Catholic Church as the "great and abominable church" of 1 Nephi 13–14 and Revelation 17. In an article in the January 1988 *Ensign*, BYU professor Stephen E. Robinson pointed out that Roman Catholicism is not, nor could it be, the "great and abominable church" of the Bible and the Book of Mormon because the great and abominable church spoken of in scripture *caused* the apostasy of the first century. From a Latter-day Saint perspective, Catholicism's arrival on the scene occurred too late for it to fit the definition.[4] In addition, its influence in the world is too good, and its intent too spiritual, to qualify it as one of the devil's primary instruments employed to destroy God's work upon the earth. Thus, believers in the restored gospel should never suggest that the Catholic Church is the great and abominable church. Such a claim is offensive, historically untenable, and theologically inaccurate.

A fifth suggested practice for interacting with Roman Catholics deals with understanding how the Church influences the day-to-day life of Catholics. Asking Catholic friends about their congregation, their involvement in it, what they love about it, and how it blesses them or their family can be a good way to start getting to know what they feel about the Church and how it serves them in their quest to be closer to God. Asking them about traditions they have for major holidays or feast days, like Christmas or Easter, can also be a great

---

4. Stephen E. Robinson, "Warring against the Saints of God," *Ensign*, Jan. 1988, 34–39.

way to understand how their faith shapes their lives. Some congregations hold an annual festival in honor of the parish's saint (such as St. Joseph's Catholic Church). Attending such a celebration is a good, informal way to show support for a Catholic friend, make some new acquaintances, and have fun in a casual and entertaining environment. Attending an event like this will give you a better sense of parish life and will send a positive message to Catholic friends that you care about understanding the things they care about.

Finally, as some Latter-day Saints already recognize, it is important to remember that our faith, like all of Christianity, owes Roman Catholics a great deal. In his 2006 article "Catholicism's Contribution to God's Plan," Latter-day Saint scholar Gerald Hansen Jr. offered a number of ways in which the Catholic Church blessed the Christian world throughout history:

1. For centuries, "Catholicism was the standard and disseminator of moral standards in Europe and other parts of the world."
2. It "kept alive for 2,000 years the idea of Jesus as the Savior of the world."
3. "The New Testament" likely would "not exist without the Catholic Church."
4. "Music as we know it in the West began its development in the Catholic mass."
5. "Art in the West was kept alive and developed . . . mostly through the Church."
6. "Universities were essentially a Catholic invention."
7. "Catholicism engendered a mindset that made modern science possible."
8. "Monks . . . copied books, and kept learning alive during times of illiteracy."[5]

Whereas members of The Church of Jesus Christ of Latter-day Saints tend to heavily emphasize the positive aspects of the Protestant Reformation in preparing the world for the Restoration, many events in Catholic history prepared the world for the coming forth of the fulness of the gospel of Jesus Christ through the prophet Joseph Smith. Thus, we should not be dismissive of the many important contributions of the Catholic Church and its members to the world, to faith, and to the Restoration of the fullness of the gospel of Jesus Christ.

---

5. Gerald Hansen, Jr., "Catholicism's Contribution to God's Plan," in *Perspective* Volume 6, Number 2 (Autumn 2006): 84–97.

12

Appreciation for Latter-day Saint Beliefs and Practices

By Dr. Mathew N. Schmalz

Whenever I reflect upon my holy envy of Latter-day Saint beliefs and practices, I recall the vision of the tree of life as given to Lehi (see 1 Nephi 8). I wonder whether I, a Catholic, would be considered one of those in the great and spacious building—not jeering but fascinated and wondering whether there could be any way to span the river of water between where I stood and the ground supporting the rod of iron. I have never lived in an area with a substantial Latter-day Saint community, so I still have much to learn about the rhythms and nuances of daily and weekly life for Latter-day Saints. Until recently, my primary points of engagement with the traditions of the Church of Jesus Christ have been abstract and theological in nature. In this chapter I initially look to the Book of Mormon and the Doctrine and Covenants to shape my understandings of the religious themes embodied in life as a member of the Church of Jesus Christ.

The Closeness of the Divine

Following his father's vision, Nephi also had vision of the tree of life (see 1 Nephi 11–14) that is more extensive in prophetic specificity. In a particularly dramatic section, the angel asked Nephi, "Knowest thou the condescension of God?" And Nephi replied, "I know that he loveth his children; nevertheless I do not know the meaning of all things" (1 Nephi 11:16–17).

In contemporary usage, "condescension" has a negative connotation associated with haughtiness or a patronizing attitude. But, in its earlier meaning and usage, it refers to coming down or acquiescing. Within the Latter-day Saint tradition, as I understand it, the condescension of God—the divine coming down to dwell among us—becomes particularly profound trough temple ordinances. Especially in temple sealings of marriages for time and eternity, as well as in proxy baptism, there is a tangible connection made—in and through divine love—between this life and the life that follows. Latter-day Saint temple worship has similarities to Catholic beliefs and practices: Catholicism too has a rich ritual life, with its own sacraments that make God's love real and meaningful; and Catholics pray for the dead and souls in purgatory, forging a connection between this life and the next. But even if one chooses instead to emphasize the overall differences between Catholic and Latter-day Saint understandings of God's plan of salvation, ritual structure of the Church of Jesus Christ still points to a coherent and powerful way of conceptualizing how God may touch and sanctify human life both in the here and now as well as in the life that continues beyond the veil of earthly death.

Certainly, for me as a Catholic, Latter-day Saint temples retain an aura of mystery. But, as I consider the temple and its ordinances, they collectively point to Christians' shared understanding of repentance and conversion. When King Benjamin speaks of how the "natural man is an enemy to God" (Mosiah 3:19), I hear him calling each and every one of us to move beyond our natural inclinations in order to become truly righteous and holy. Some of the Book of Mormon's most powerful sections concern the repentance and conversion necessary to "put off" the natural man. For example, I find Alma's discourse on repentance and conversion (see Alma 5) particularly meaningful, especially when he speaks of the necessity of being "stripped of pride" and "of envy" (Alma 5:28–29). It is also appropriate, I think, to understand temple ordinances as a kind of labor (members themselves often refer to their participation as "temple work"), and it is by our laboring to be righteous and holy, together with the action of divine mercy, that we come "to sing the song of redeeming love" (Alma 5:26). From my Catholic perspective, the notion of the divine as being a close and loving presence is not new or alien. But the Latter-day Saint articulation of this aspect of

Christian faith is particularly persuasive in how it relates sacred texts and ritual to understanding how our "garments [may] be cleansed and made white through the blood of Christ" (Alma 5:27).

Both Catholic and Latter-day Saint spiritualities emphasize the need to become Christlike. For Catholics, it is Jesus's death on the cross that is meditated upon most deeply and consistently, and many Catholic mystics and religious teachers have reflected upon what it means to unite oneself with Christ crucified. The Latter-day Saint emphasis is somewhat different. Douglas Davies, a prominent Anglican scholar of the theology and practice of the Church of Jesus Christ, argues that it is Jesus's "inner crucifixion" that is most relevant for understanding their spirituality. This inner crucifixion comes in the Garden of Gethsemane, where Jesus vicariously experienced the totality of human sin and suffering—a point made most poignantly and persuasively for me by Stephen E. Robinson in his book *Believing Christ*. Crucial then is Jesus's choice—His agency—to do as His Father wills. Accordingly, Latter-day Saint ethics consistently maintains the importance of making good decisions, of "choosing the right."

Detractors of the Catholic tradition have often said that Catholicism values human works at the expense of God's grace. In the view of such detractors, Catholics believe that they can essentially "earn" their salvation in a straightforward way, simply by doing good deeds. But for me, what becomes apparent in both the Catholic and Latter-day Saint conceptions of the divine is that there is a delicate and complementary balance between human and divine agency. Reflecting on the understandings of the Church of Jesus Christ with respect to God or the Godhead thus allows me to better appreciate and understand the many ways we as human beings can be elevated and empowered by divine love.

Building Community

When I was having lunch with BYU professors during a conference, I asked my colleague sitting next to me what he thought I should convey about Latter-day Saints to my majority Catholic students. He replied, "Our unity." The idea of "the gathering together" of Zion (Doctrine and Covenants 115:6) is indeed captivating for many outsiders interested in life and culture of members of the Church of Jesus Christ. From my outsider's perspective, I can clearly see a strong sense of community among Latter-day Saints—a sense of community that I admire and, admittedly, envy.

As I grew up Catholic in the 1970s, my life was enriched by priests who were family friends in addition to being officiants at Sunday Mass. Times have definitely changed: Catholic parishes have merged and grown larger in order to deal with a shortage of priests, and it is much harder to develop a personal relationship with priests and fellow parishioners in such a context. Even more sadly, the reverberations of the sexual abuse crisis can still be felt at all levels of Catholic life.

Given the changes in Catholic life in the last few decades, I cannot help but cast an envious eye toward what seems to be Latter-day Saint success in building a wholesome and encompassing community life. For example, when I look at how the Church of Jesus Christ has organized wards, there seems to be an overriding concern that wards not become too large and lose their sense of close-knit community. The establishment of student wards seems to be a creative way to foster strong bonds among Latter-day Saints who are at similar stages in life. All of this, combined with the numerous activities and opportunities for collective service, creates a powerful sense of community that any contemporary Catholic would understandably find attractive.

The history of the Latter-day Saints also testifies to their desire to build a broader sense of community based upon service and love. There were early Latter-day Saint attempts to keep the law of consecration by sharing property (see Doctrine and Covenants 42:30–39), which I look upon with respect, especially when seen through Catholic understandings of the common good. The present-day Church's welfare program seems to me to be an effective way to balance individual responsibility and community needs. Even tithing, which might be off-putting to some commentators, demonstrates a deep commitment to community based upon shared sacrifice.

But it is probably the emphasis of the Church of Jesus Christ upon society's most crucial element—the family—that most resonates with Catholic values. Of course, in the tradition of the Church of Jesus Christ, the family is not just a unit of society; it is a fundamental unit of salvation. From a Catholic perspective, what is striking about Latter-day Saint understandings of the importance of the family is not simply that we will be with our loved ones after death, but that the family has a fundamental, and indeed indivisible, place in God plan. Even something as seemingly simple as the practice of family home evening testifies to the admirable focus on strengthening and deepening family closeness and love.

I am grateful to teach at an institution where many students pursue Church service opportunities after graduation. I myself did a year of service for the Catholic Church before I entered college, and it was transformative for me. So when I look at how many Latter-day Saints become missionaries, I recognize it as a deep and profound experience that brings Latter-day Saints together to engage the wider world. It is interesting too, for me as a scholar, to see how Latter-day Saints portray missionary work in similarly heroic terms as in the Catholic tradition. One can read about the experiences of Lehi and Nephi among the Lamanites in Helaman 5, for example, and find a narrative that would strike familiar chords for a Catholic reader. Of course, it is important to recognize that missionary activity by any denomination will always have critics, since there are many ways in which evangelization can be coercive or manipulative. But King Benjamin, when he specifically speaks of rearing children, sets what seems to me to be the proper orientation guidance for missionary work as well: to teach us "to love one another, and to serve one another" (Mosiah 4:15). President Spencer W. Kimball also emphasized missionary work not as toil but as sharing joy. As a Catholic, I deeply respect what I see as the shared experiences and potential for self-transformation made possible by the Church of Jesus Christ's commitment to missionary outreach.

Optimism and Vitality

Yale professor and literary theorist Harold Bloom is the most often-quoted non-affiliated commentator on Joseph Smith. In a particularly pithy formulation, Bloom wrote that Joseph Smith gave us an understanding of "a more human god, and a more divine man."[1] While Catholic and Latter-day Saint interpretations of the plan of salvation differ substantially, I would echo Bloom's admiring comments regarding Joseph Smith's prophetic vision.

Seen through my Catholic lens, Joseph Smith's vision seems breathtakingly expansive and optimistic. In the non-canonical but nonetheless important King Follett discourse, Joseph provided words of comfort by saying

---

1. Harold Bloom, *The American Religion: The Emergence of a Post-Christian Nation* (New York: Simon & Schuster, 1992), 100.

we will meet our deceased loved ones again "in the morn of the celestial world."[2] He echoed and extended the content of visions previously given to him that reveal and affirm the existence of celestial, terrestrial, and telestial kingdoms, and identify those who shall enter them (see Doctrine and Covenants 76). Joseph also went further to proclaim that salvation is open to all except those who have committed the unpardonable sin against the Holy Ghost. But Joseph's understanding of this sin is particularly thought-provoking when he said that it is to have "the heavens opened unto them, & know God" and then turn from that and fight against God. Thus, for Joseph, to deny the Holy Ghost meant you needed to have seen God or Christ or an angel and consequently know that God lives and that the gospel is true—and then come out in "open war" against that knowledge.[3] From a Catholic perspective, there is a heady and wholesome optimism in Joseph's understanding of God's plan of salvation that sheds an intriguing light on the gospel passage "My Father's house has many rooms" (John 14:2, NIV).

In speaking of my holy envy of Latter-day Saints, it is all too easy to evoke common stereotypes such as that Latter-day Saints are clean-cut, polite, and hardworking. But there does seem to me to be a vitality to life as a member of the Church of Jesus Christ that, at least to me, reflects one of Joseph's key points in the King Follett discourse, namely that "all the spirits that God ever sent into the world are susceptible of enlargement."[4] In recent years, I have been blessed by my friendships with Latter-day Saints who have given me hope and support during difficult times as they give witness to the love that Heavenly Father has for each and every one of us. While Catholics and Latter-day Saints have theologies that differ on many points, I have found that reflecting upon the distinctiveness of our respective religious visions—and where they intersect—can be a powerful way to enlarge and improve our Christian faith as we together journey with Jesus.

---

2. Joseph Smith, Discourse, 7 April 1844, as reported by Wilford Woodruff, https://www.josephsmithpapers.org/paper-summary/discourse-7-april-1844-as-reported-by-wilford-woodruff.
3. Joseph Smith, Discourse, 7 April 1844, as reported by Wilford Woodruff, https://www.josephsmithpapers.org/paper-summary/discourse-7-april-1844-as-reported-by-wilford-woodruff.
4. Joseph Smith, Discourse, 7 April 1844, as reported by William Clayton, https://www.josephsmithpapers.org/paper-summary/discourse-7-april-1844-as-reported-by-william-clayton.

Glossary of Catholic Terms

Important Catholic terms not appearing in this text are marked with an asterisk (*).

Absolution: A ritual formula for forgiving sins.

Apostles' Creed: One of the earliest statements of Christian doctrine, traditionally believed to express the beliefs of the apostles. It affirms faith in God, the Father; Jesus, the Son; and the Holy Spirit.

Annulment: The abrogation or reversal of a marriage because the marriage was invalid due to inconsistencies with Church law.

Apocrypha: See "Deuterocanonical Books."

Archbishop: A bishop of the highest rank, who is responsible for the bishops within his archdiocese (a larger geographical area encompassing many dioceses).

Ash Wednesday: A day of fasting and penance that begins the period of Lent. During Ash Wednesday services, the priest makes the sign of the cross, with ashes, on the forehead and says, "Remember that you are dust and unto dust you shall return."

Assumption of the Virgin Mary: The dogma, or infallible doctrine, promulgated by Pope Pius XII in 1950, that Mary was "assumed" or taken body and soul into heaven.

Baptism: From the Greek word "to dip" or "immerse"; baptism is the central rite of membership in the Catholic Church. In Roman Catholicism, baptism is performed in infancy, though adult converts are baptized as well. The central element of the rite is pouring water over the forehead.

Beatific Vision: "Immediate knowledge" or vision of God experienced in heaven by those who are saved.

Bishop: The leader of an administrative district called a diocese. Bishops are chosen by the pope.

Blessed: One level below sainthood. A blessed is someone who led a life of heroic virtue and by whose intercession one miracle has taken place. Martyrs and confessors (those who were put to death or tortured for their faith) do not need a miracle associated with them to become blessed. The process for being named "blessed" is called "beatification."

Canonization: The process by which a deceased person is made into a saint and has a feast day entered into the Church's calendar, which is called "the canon."

Cardinal: A Church leader (usually an archbishop) who is appointed by the pope to join the college of cardinals, the pope's principal advisers.

Catholic Worker Movement*: Founded by Dorothy Day and Peter Maurin in 1933, the movement is composed of self-governing communities devoted to service of the poor.

Church: The term is sometimes used more broadly to denote the unity of all Christians. However, the Catholic Church understands itself, as a church, to be the institution and community established and willed by God for the salvation of humankind.

Clergy: Ordained ministers such as bishops, priests, and deacons, who have authority to administer the sacraments.

Common Good: Individual and social commitment to what is good for the human community; a fundamental principle of Catholic social teaching.

Confirmation: A sacrament following baptism in which a Catholic is "confirmed" in her or his faith and membership in the Church. A candidate for confirmation is sponsored by another Catholic, and the confirmation itself is sealed by being anointed on the forehead with oil by a bishop.

Consecrated: Nuns, clergy, and laypersons who have taken a public vow of poverty, chastity, and obedience.

Council of Nicaea (AD 325): Convened by the Roman emperor Constantine to resolve issues concerning the divine and human natures of Christ and the overall status of the Trinity. This council produced the Nicene Creed.

Counter-Reformation*: Period beginning with the Council of Trent (1545–1563) that inaugurated responses to Protestantism in the form of evangelization and missionary activity. This period is also associated with Catholic expansion in Asia and the rise of the Society of Jesus, also known as "the Jesuits."

Crucifix: A cross with a depiction of Jesus.

Deacon: An ordained member of the Church, of lesser rank than priest. Deacons are allowed to preach, witness marriage services, and conduct wake and funeral services. Married men may be deacons.

Deuterocanonical Books: Literally "second canon," these are parts of the Old Testament accepted as authentic by the Catholic and Greek Orthodox Churches but not by many other Christian denominations. These books are also called "the Apocrypha" and include the books of Tobit, Judith, Baruch, Sirach, 1 Maccabees, 2 Maccabees, and Wisdom of Solomon, as well as additions to Esther and Daniel.

Diaconate: The office of deacon, or the group of clergy who hold this office within the Church.

Diocese: An area of Church governance, led and administered by a bishop; comparable to a Latter-day Saint stake.

Dogma: A binding, divinely revealed truth, associated with a decree made by a council of the whole Church or an ex cathedra statement of the pope in which infallibility is invoked.

Edict of Milan (AD 313)*: A letter signed and promulgated by Emperors Constantine and Licinius that established religious toleration in the Roman Empire.

Encyclical*: A papal letter that contains official teaching.

Eucharist: From the Greek word for "thanksgiving"; the sacramental celebration of the sacrificial offering of Jesus Christ in which the Eucharistic elements of bread and wine become His body and blood.

Excommunication*: Expulsion from the Catholic Church for a particular offense like heresy. An individual bishop or the pope can pronounce excommunication. This sanction is rarely used in the present day.

Extraordinary Magisterium: Infallible teachings made either through specifically defined pronouncements of the pope or through a council approved by the pope.

Extreme Unction: The sacrament of anointing of the sick with oil by a priest.

First Vatican Council (1869–1870): A council held in Rome, convened by Pope Pius IX and including bishops from the entire Church. The First Vatican Council proclaimed the dogma of papal infallibility.

Genuflect: The act of lowering one's body by bending one knee to the ground during worship.

Good Friday: The solemn commemoration of Christ's crucifixion.

Grace: The unmerited help that God provides human beings to draw close to Him.

Hail Mary: A prayer expressing praise for and asking help of the Virgin Mary.

Holy Orders: The sacrament of ordination to the priesthood by a bishop. The priesthood in Roman Catholicism is reserved for males.

Holy Thursday: The commemoration of the Last Supper, marked by the priest washing the feet of twelve congregants.

Host: A consecrated or blessed Eucharistic wafer, which is always made of unleavened bread.

Immaculate Conception: The dogma that Mary was conceived without original sin.

Inculturation: Adapting Catholic religious practice to local culture.

Infallibility/Infallible: A pronouncement incapable of being erroneous, as when a pope speaks ex cathedra or "from the throne" regarding a question of faith or morals. Infallibility is also understood to apply to proclamations made by councils of the entire Church.

Jesuits*: Less formal name for "the Society of Jesus," established by Ignatius of Loyola in 1540. Jesuit spirituality is characterized by an emphasis on discernment and service in the world, particularly through education and missionary work.

Laity: Non-ordained or non-consecrated members of the Catholic Church; often called "the faithful" or "the people of God."

Lector: A reader during worship, often a layperson.

Lent: Forty days of fasting in preparation for celebrating the resurrection of Jesus Christ. Lent begins on Ash Wednesday and ends on Holy Saturday, the day before Easter.

Liturgy: The set of rituals including the celebration of Mass and the other sacraments; the formula for public worship of God and proclamation of the gospel.

Magisterium: The teaching office and authority of the Catholic Church.

Matrimony: The sacrament of marriage, which in Catholicism is considered to be possible only between one man and one woman and is binding for life.

Mass: The liturgy of the Word, which includes readings from the Old and New Testament and the celebration of the Eucharist. Catholics are required to go to Mass on Sundays, and some go every day.

Nicene Creed: The creed that summarizes the orthodox faith of Catholicism and is used in the liturgy of most Christian churches. It was adopted at the first Council of Nicaea in AD 325.

Ordinary Magisterium: Teachings of the Catholic Church that are not necessarily infallible unless they are taught consistently over time by the bishops of the entire church in communion with the pope. The ordinary magisterium is the foundation for the extraordinary magisterium.

Original Sin: The disposition to sin inherent in all human beings, inherited as a consequence of the disobedience of Adam and Eve in the Garden of Eden.

Parish: The most basic and smallest unit of the Catholic Church, similar in size to a Latter-day Saint ward.

Particular Judgment: The immediate judgment after death of those who die before the Second Coming of Christ.

Patron Saint: A saint who is a special advocate of a particular cause, place, occupation, or person.

Pope: The spiritual and administrative head of the Catholic Church on earth. The pope is considered to be the successor of the apostle Peter and the representative of Christ.

Prayer of the Faithful: A part of the Mass during which the congregation makes known its prayers for the world, the Church, the nation, and other specific intentions, particularly for the wellbeing of the sick and oppressed.

Priest: An ordained minister of the gospel. Priests can only be male and are usually addressed as "Father."

Prudential Judgment: A decision or evaluation that is not infallible.

Purgatory: Intermediate state before entering heaven, in which the last vestiges of sin are "purged" or cleansed.

Real Presence: The actual presence of the body and blood of Jesus Christ under the appearance of the bread and wine of the Eucharist.

Reconciliation: The sacrament in which a Catholic confesses her or his sins to a priest and, if truly penitent, is forgiven.

Rerum Novarum (1891)*: Latin for "of new things"; an encyclical, or papal letter, promulgated by Pope Leo XIII that affirmed workers' rights and called for a more just ordering of society.

Rite: A ceremonial practice of a church or group of churches. May also refer to a group within the Catholic Church with its own distinctive liturgical and theological tradition that nevertheless accepts the universal authority of the pope.

Rosary: A string of beads used to count recitations of prayers such as Our Father and the Hail Mary.

Sacrament: A ritual or sign instituted by Christ that provides grace.

Sacramental: An act or object relating to the sacraments.

Saint: A person who has led a life of heroic virtue and whose intercession has resulted in two miracles. The formal process for naming a saint, called "canonization," can only begin after the person is deceased.

Second Vatican Council (1962–1965): A council of the entire Church convened by Pope John XXIII; also known as Vatican II. The Second Vatican Council established a more conciliatory posture to contemporary culture and allowed the Mass to be celebrated in local languages instead of Latin.

Sign of the Cross: A gesture that symbolizes both the cross and the Trinity, made by outlining a cross from the forehead to the chest and to each shoulder while repeating, aloud or silently, "In the name of the Father, Son, and Holy Spirit."

Sign of Peace: A part of the Mass during which congregants wish each other peace, usually with a handshake and the words "peace be with you."

Soteriology: Religious doctrines, beliefs, or theology about salvation, including how one is saved and what life after death will look like.

Subordinationism: The belief that the Son and the Holy Spirit are subordinate to God the Father, and dependent upon the Father for Their existence. The New Testament and many early Christians were subordinationists; and a controversy over subordinationism led to the First Council of Nicaea (AD 325).

Subsidiarity: The principle in Catholic social thought that nothing should be done by or at a higher authority or level that can be done by or at a lower authority or level.

Tabernacle: A special container or "dwelling place" near the altar, in which the consecrated Eucharistic host is "reserved" or kept.

Transubstantiation: The belief that the bread and wine, when consecrated at the Mass, become the body and blood of Jesus Christ.

Triduum: The period beginning on the evening of Holy Thursday and ending on the evening of Easter Sunday.

Trinity: One God in three divine Persons: God, the Father; Jesus, the Son; and The Holy Spirit. These three Persons are coeternal and one in substance.

Venerable: The title given to a deceased person whose life has been judged to be heroic and virtuous and who is being considered for beatification and eventual sainthood.

Important Dates and Events in Catholicism

The history of the Catholic Church extends over two thousand years, and a full discussion of Catholicism's historical course has filled many long and complex volumes. Below are some of the important dates and events in Catholic history, up to the present day.

It is important to understand that Catholicism developed out of persecution (during the Roman Empire) to become aligned with political and imperial powers for more than a thousand years—up until the Protestant Reformation. Catholic responses to the Protestant Reformation involved internal efforts to address religious and doctrinal abuses and also external efforts in the form of evangelization and missionary activity. In the twentieth and twenty-first centuries, the Catholic Church has both engaged and resisted prominent social and cultural trends and practices. As of this writing in 2024, the Catholic Church has over one billion members, with the majority residing in the "global South."

Catholicism and Imperial Power

- 313   Edict of Milan, which began toleration of Christianity in the Roman Empire.
- 325   Council of Nicaea, which defined the Trinity in which the Father, Son, and Holy Spirit are considered equally divine.
- 547   Death of Benedict of Nursia, founder of the monastery Monte Cassino and the beginnings of the monastic movement that preserved Christian learning.
- 1054   Schism that split Christianity into Eastern and Western branches.
- 1085   Death of Pope Gregory VII, who enforced celibacy requirements for priests.

Middle Ages

- 1226   Death of St. Francis of Assisi, who inspired Catholics through his humility and love of the natural world.
- 1274   Deaths of St. Thomas Aquinas and St. Bonaventure, who drew upon Greek philosophy to advance and deepen Christian theology and spirituality.
- 1390   Death of St. Catherine of Siena, a Catholic mystic who probed the depths of the individual experience of Jesus Christ.

Reformation and Counter-Reformation

1561   Excommunication of Martin Luther, a former monk and leading figure of the Protestant Reformation.

1545–1563
The Council of Trent, the beginning of the "Counter-Reformation" in which Catholicism opposed Protestantism through preaching and missionary work.

1556   Death of St. Ignatius of Loyola, founder of "the Society of Jesus" or Jesuits.

Modern Era

1869–1870
The First Vatican Council, which defined the infallibility of the pope.

1903   Death of Pope Leo XIII, who published the encyclical or papal letter "Rerum Novarum" (Of New Things), which called for a more just society.

1962–1965
Second Vatican Council, convened by Pope John XXIII, which made significant changes in Catholic liturgy, including allowing Mass to be celebrated in local languages instead of Latin.

1975   Death of St. Josemaría Escrivá, founder of Opus Dei, an institution of the Church emphasizing holiness in the ordinary life.

1980   Death of Dorothy Day, co-founder of the Catholic Worker Movement.

1997   Death of St. Teresa of Calcutta, founder of the Missionaries of Charity.

2005   Death of St. John Paul II, first non-Italian pope in four hundred years.

2011   Resignation of Pope Benedict XVI, first papal resignation in six hundred years; election of Pope Francis, the first pope from the global South.

Important Catholic Figures

Augustine of Hippo (354–430): The most influential theologian of the early Church fathers, authoring *Confessions* and *The City of God*, with extensive writing about human depravity, the Fall of Adam and Eve, human freedom, just war, mortal goodness, preexistence, the division and inferiority of the physical body and world, and many other topics.

Benedict of Nursia (480–547): Founder of the Western monastic tradition and of Monte Cassino, one of the most important monasteries in the Catholic world; often credited with writing the Rule of St. Benedict, an important monastic code.

Benedict XVI (b. 1927-2022): Primary author of the Catholic Catechism as Joseph Ratzinger; elected to the papacy in 2005 and resigned in 2013; known for his sophisticated theological writings and papal encyclicals.

Bonaventure (1221–1274): Medieval philosopher known for engaging with Greek philosophy, particularly that of Plato. He was canonized in 1542.

Catherine of Siena (1347–1380): Italian mystic who claimed a spiritual marriage with Jesus Christ. Her *Dialogue* is considered a classic of Catholic spirituality. She was canonized in 1461.

Dorothy Day (1897–1980): Catholic convert, social activist, and co-founder of the Catholic Worker Movement.

Francis of Assisi (d. 1226): Beloved Catholic mystic whose humility and love for nature and for the poor continue to inspire Catholics.

Gregory VII (1015–1085): Reforming pope who excommunicated the Holy Roman Emperor, Henry VI, and enforced the celibacy requirement for priests.

Ignatius of Loyola (1491–1556): A member of Spanish nobility who renounced his weapons and offered them up to the Virgin Mary. He was the founder of "the Society of Jesus," or Jesuits, and his *Spiritual Exercises* is foundational for Catholic spirituality.

John Paul II (1920–2005): Karol Józef Wojtyła, first non-Italian pope in over four hundred years. Known for his advocacy of "a culture of life" and his strong opposition to communism.

Josemaría Escrivá (1902–1975): Founder of the Catholic institution Opus Dei (the work of God), which includes both clergy and laypeople who seek to find sanctification in ordinary life. He was canonized in 2002.

Leo XIII (1810–1903): Vincenzo Gioacchino Raffaele Luigi Pecci, author of the influential papal encyclical *Rerum Novarum* ("Of New Things").

Pope Francis (b. 1936): Jorge Maria Bergoglio, elected to the papacy in 2013. The first pope from Argentina and the global South, known for his commitment to the poor and care of the natural world. Pope Francis is also a member of the Society of Jesus.

Teresa of Calcutta (1910–1997): Anjezë Gonxhe Bojaxhiu, known as Mother Teresa; founder of the religious order Missionaries of Charity, which ministers to the sick and dying. She was canonized in 2016.

Thomas Aquinas (1225–1274): Medieval philosopher known for engaging with Greek philosophy, particularly that of Aristotle. His multi-volume work *Summa Theologica* is still influential in Catholic philosophy and theology. He was canonized in 1542.

Significant Locations in Roman Catholicism

Site	Location	Significance
Basilica of Our Lady of Peace	Yamoussoukro, Ivory Coast	World's largest church
Bethlehem	Israel	Place of Jesus's birth
Black Nazarene	Manila, Philippines	Famous statue and feast
Chartres	France	Site of important cathedral
Christ the Redeemer	Corcovado, Brazil	Important statue of Jesus Christ
Croagh Patrick	County Mayo, Ireland	Mountain sacred to St. Patrick
Fátima Shrine	Fátima, Portugal	Site of apparition of Virgin Mary; pilgrimage site
Goa	India	"Rome of the East"; headquarters for Catholic mission efforts in Asia in the sixteenth through eighteenth centuries
Jasna Gora	Częstochowa, Poland	Monastery and shrine
Jerusalem	Israel	Place of Jesus's death
Knock Shrine	Knock, Ireland	Site of apparition of Virgin Mary; shrine
LaSallette	France	Site of apparition of the Virgin Mary
Lourdes	France	Site of apparition of the Virgin Mary; pilgrimage site
Mont St. Michel	Normandy, France	Famous island monastery
Monte Cassino Monastery	Monte Cassino, Italy	Famous monastery
Munyonyo Martyrs Shrine	Namugongo, Uganda	Shrine to nineteenth-century Ugandan martyrs
Notre Dame	Paris, France	Important cathedral
Our Lady of Good Health	Vailankanni, India	Site of apparition of the Virgin Mary; pilgrimage site
Our Lady of Guadalupe	Mexico City, Mexico	Site of apparition of the Virgin Mary; pilgrimage site
Rio de Janeiro Cathedral	Rio de Janeiro, Brazil	Important church in the world's most populous majority-Catholic country
Vatican City	Rome, Italy	Nation-state headquarters of the Catholic Church

Catholic Prayers and Creedal Statements

Apostles' Creed

I believe in God, the Father almighty, creator of heaven and earth. I believe in Jesus Christ, his only Son, our Lord. He was conceived by the power of the Holy Spirit and born of the Virgin Mary. He suffered under Pontius Pilate, was crucified, died, and was buried. He descended to the dead. On the third day he rose again. He ascended into heaven, and is seated at the right hand of the Father. He will come again to judge the living and the dead. I believe in the Holy Spirit, the holy Catholic Church, the communion of the saints, the forgiveness of sins, the resurrection of the body, and the life everlasting. Amen

Hail Mary

Hail Mary, full of grace, the Lord is with thee. Blessed art thou amongst women, and blessed is the fruit of thy womb, Jesus. Holy Mary, Mother of God, pray for us sinners, now and at the hour of our death. Amen.

Lord's Prayer/Our Father

Our Father who art in heaven, Hallowed be thy name. Thy kingdom come. Thy will be done, on earth as it is in heaven. Give us this day our daily bread, and forgive us our trespasses, as we forgive those who trespass against us, and lead us not into temptation, but deliver us from evil.

Nicene Creed

I believe in one God, the Father almighty, maker of heaven and earth, of all things visible and invisible. I believe in one Lord Jesus Christ, the Only Begotten Son of God, born of the Father before all ages. God from God, Light from Light, true God from true God, begotten, not made, consubstantial with the Father; through him all things were made. For us men and for our salvation he came down from heaven, and by the Holy Spirit was incarnate of the Virgin Mary, and became man. For our sake he was crucified under Pontius Pilate, he suffered death and was buried, and rose again on the third day in accordance with the Scriptures. He ascended into heaven and is seated at the right hand of the Father. He will come again in glory to judge the living and the dead and his kingdom will have no end. I believe in the Holy Spirit, the Lord, the giver of life, who proceeds from the Father and the Son, who with the Father and the Son is adored and glorified, who has spoken through the prophets. I believe in one, holy, catholic and apostolic Church. I confess one Baptism for the forgiveness of sins and I look forward to the resurrection of the dead and the life of the world to come. Amen.

Comparison of Catholic and Church of Jesus Christ Doctrine

	Roman Catholic	Church of Jesus Christ
Trinity/ Godhead	The Father, Son, and Holy Spirit are one God existing in three Persons, simultaneously united in substance but distinct in personhood or roles. "Substance" is traditionally understood to mean "nature" and, thus, the three Persons of the Trinity are not one modalistic Being. Rather, they are three distinct Persons who share the same divine nature, and who—through their divine relationship—constitute "one God." The three Persons of the Trinity are coeternal and coequal.	The Father, Son, and Holy Spirit constitute a singular Godhead. They are one in nature but utterly distinct in personhood and roles in the Godhead. The Son and the Holy Spirit are subordinate to the Father because the Father is the source of the Son and Holy Ghost. Thus, the Son and Spirit are not coequal or coeternal with the Father. The Father existed as divine and exalted prior to the Son and the Holy Spirit joining the Godhead.
Jesus	Jesus is the only begotten of the Father, who is coeternal and consubstantial with the Father. Being "begotten" does not mean that Jesus had a beginning but, instead, means that He took His place next to the Father in the Holy Trinity. However, Jesus and the Father have always existed as coequal in the Trinity.	Jesus is the only begotten of the Father, which means that there was a time when the Father existed as God but Jesus did not yet exist as God's spirit offspring or Son. Jesus subordinates Himself to the Father in all things and fulfills the Father's will in all things. Jesus is a member of the Godhead, but there was a time when He was not, as the Godhead had not yet been organized or established.
Holy Spirit	The Holy Spirit is coeternal and consubstantial with the Father and the Son. He proceeds forth from the Father and the Son. He serves as the presence of the Father in the world.	The Holy Ghost is one of the spirit offspring of God the Father and, thus, is not coeternal with the Father but subordinate to the Father. While Latter-day Saints don't speak of the "procession" of the Spirit, it is consistent with their doctrine to say He proceeds from the Father, not from the Father and the Son. He acts on behalf of the Father and serves as the presence of the Father in the world.

	Roman Catholic	Church of Jesus Christ
Mary	Mary is the "Mother of God," and the greatest of the saints. She is the mediatrix, which means she plays an intercessory role in humankind's access to Jesus's redemptive act. She was a perpetual virgin and lived a completely sinless life. Jesus is the only child she bore. Upon her death, she was taken up body and soul into heaven. This is taken to be a sign of the bodily resurrection promised at the end of time.	Mary is the mother of Jesus, and one of the greatest—if not the greatest—of Heavenly Father's female spirit offspring. She lived a faithful life, reared a family with Joseph, died, and was buried. While her life is worthy of emulation, she is not to be prayed to or appealed to, and she plays no mediatory role in the salvation of God's children.
Church	The Roman Catholic Church understands itself to be the church that contains the fulness of truth, based upon an apostolic tradition that goes back to Jesus and the apostles. However, other Christian denominations and non-Christian religions may reflect a measure of truth. Non-Catholics and non-Christians may thus be saved. The Catholic Church strongly encourages interreligious dialogue and appreciating what is good and true in all religions.	The Church of Jesus Christ of Latter-day Saints is God's authorized organization on the earth. While it has a fuller portion of God's truth, it holds that other religions have some measure of truth and are not void of the influence of God. From the foundations of the world, the preaching of the gospel in the spirit world and vicarious ordinances for the dead were part of God's plan of salvation, making it possible for those who did not have the fullness of the gospel during mortality to be saved. The restored gospel is the bearer of the keys necessary for valid salvific ordinances.
Hierarchy	There are three levels of ordained clerical hierarchy: bishops, priests, and deacons. The pope is a bishop who is the administrative head of the Church and is understood to be the successor to the apostle Peter.	There are numerous layers of ecclesiastical hierarchy, from prophet (president of the Church) down to deacons. Each has a different level of priesthood authority and a different stewardship. The higher ecclesiastical offices hold broader authority than do the lower ones. The president of the Church is believed to hold apostolic authority and keys, which can be traced back to Jesus through an unbroken line of apostolic succession.

	Roman Catholic	Church of Jesus Christ
Priesthood	Any Catholic priesthood office, from parish priest and above, requires years of academic training. Not all priests supervise a parish; some have different ministries, such as being a hospital chaplain. Additionally, some priests are members of religious orders. Religious orders are groups of priests who have taken additional vows within that community and have a special ministry.	Any Latter-day Saint priesthood office, from deacon to apostle, comes only after established worthiness and expressed faith in the major doctrines of the Church. In the case of offices like high priest, patriarch, or apostle, ordination to these offices comes only after years of experience in Church service and through manifest faithfulness.
Sacraments	The Roman Catholic Church acknowledges seven sacraments: (1) baptism, (2) confirmation, (3) the Eucharist, (4) penance and reconciliation, (5) extreme unction, or anointing of the sick, (6) holy orders, and (7) matrimony. All sacraments are understood to be the primary rituals through which the faithful receive God's grace. Baptism, confirmation, and the Eucharist are traditionally understood to be sacraments of initiation. Unlike all other sacraments, holy orders can be received only by men. Neither holy orders, anointing of the sick, nor matrimony are requisite for salvation.	While The Church of Jesus Christ of Latter-day Saints only officially refers to one ordinance as "the sacrament" (i.e., the sacrament of the Lord's Supper), it has many sacramental ordinances: (1) naming and blessing a child, (2) baptism, (3) confirmation, (4) the sacrament of the Lord's Supper, (5) ordination of men to an office in the priesthood, (6) the temple endowment, (7) the eternal sealing of families. Other than the naming and blessing of a child, these are traditionally seen as salvific ordinances.
Scripture	The Holy Bible, in addition to the traditions of the Roman Catholic Church (i.e., counsels, creeds, and longstanding teachings of the Church) are seen as canonical in Roman Catholicism.	The Bible, Book of Mormon, Doctrine and Covenants, and Pearl of Great Price, in addition to the traditions of the Church (i.e., official declarations, some official proclamations, certain seminal addresses of presiding authorities) are seen as authoritative and, in many cases, canonical in The Church of Jesus Christ of Latter-day Saints.

Suggested Readings on Roman Catholicism

Catechism of the Catholic Church. Double Day, 2003. Available at http://www.vatican.va/archive/ENG0015/_INDEX.HTM

Day, Dorothy. *The Long Loneliness: The Autobiography of the Legendary Catholic Social Activist.* HarperOne, 2009.

Greene, Graham. *The Power and the Glory.* Open Road Media, 2018.

Hopcke, Robert H. and Paul Schwartz. *The Little Flowers of St. Francis of Assisi: A New Translation.* New Seeds, 2006.

Johnson, Kevin Orlin. *Why Do Catholics Do That? A Guide to the Teachings and Practices of the Catholic Church.* Ballantine Books, 1995.

McBrien, Richard P. *Catholicism: New Study Edition*, revised and updated. HarperOne, 1994.

McBrien, Richard P. *The HarperCollins Encyclopedia of Catholicism.* HarperSanFrancisco, 1995.

Mother Teresa and Brian Kolodiejchuk. *Come Be My Light: The Private Writings of the Saint of Calcutta.* Image Books, 2009.

New American Bible. United States Conference of Catholic Bishops. 2002. Available at http://www.vatican.va/archive/ENG0839/_INDEX.HTM

O'Connor, Flannery. *A Prayer Journal.* Edited by W. A. Sessions. Straus and Giroux, 2013.

Pope Francis. *Laudato Si'*—On Care for Our Common Home. Our Sunday Visitor, 2015. Available at http://www.vatican.va/content/francesco/en/encyclicals/documents/papa-francesco_20150524_enciclica-laudato-si.html

Pope Francis. *The Name of God Is Mercy.* Random House, 2016.

Pope John Paul II and Joseph Durepos. *John Paul II: Lessons for Living.* Loyola Press, 2004.

Ratzinger, Joseph. *Introduction to Christianity.* Ignatius Press, 2004.

The Real Presence of Jesus Christ in the Sacrament of the Eucharist: Basic Answers and Questions. United States Conference of Catholic Bishops, 2001. Available at https://www.usccb.org/prayer-and-worship/the-mass/order-of-mass/liturgy-of-the-eucharist/the-real-presence-faqs

About the Authors

Professor Mathew N. Schmalz, PhD

Mathew N. Schmalz was born and raised in Massachusetts, where he lived until he graduated from Amherst College and attended graduate school at the University of Chicago. He is now a professor of comparative religions at the College of the Holy Cross, a Catholic liberal arts institution in Worcester, Massachusetts. He has also worked for the Catholic Church in various non-academic roles, including managing a homeless shelter in New York City and serving as a volunteer with Mother Teresa's Missionaries of Charity in India.

Dr. Schmalz has been married to his wife, Kristin, for over twenty years, and together they are raising two daughters, Anna and Katie. They are animal lovers and at various times have had goldfish, a rabbit, hermit crabs, a gecko, a large standard poodle, chickens, and a potbellied pig.

Professor Alonzo L. Gaskill, PhD

Alonzo L. Gaskill was born and raised in Jackson County, Missouri. After two decades as an active member of the Greek Orthodox Church, he became a member of The Church of Jesus Christ of Latter-day Saints and later served a mission in England. Upon his return, he earned degrees in education, philosophy, theology, and biblical studies and began a career with the Church Educational System, teaching seminary for four years in southeastern Idaho. Since 2003, he has been a professor of world religions at Brigham Young University.

Dr. Gaskill has been married to his wife, Lori, since 1989. They have five children, and three grandchildren. They currently reside in Payson, Utah.

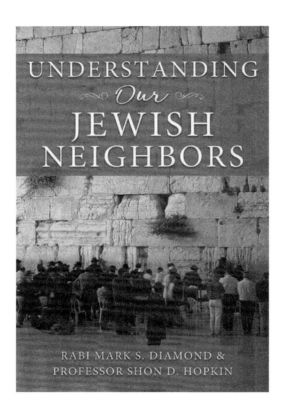

Scan to QR code to purchase
Understanding Our Jewish Neighbors
and see other books in the
Understanding Our Neighbors Series